SMART,
SUCCESSFUL &
ABUSED

SMART, SUCCESSFUL & ABUSED

The Unspoken Problem of Domestic Violence and High-Achieving Women

DR. ANGELA MAILIS

sh.
SUTHERLAND
HOUSE

TORONTO, 2019

Sutherland House
416 Moore Ave., Suite 205
Toronto, ON M4G 1C9

Sutherland House and logo are registered
trademarks of The Sutherland House Inc.

First edition, September 2019

If you are interested in inviting one of our authors to a live event or media appearance, please contact publicity@sutherlandhousebooks.com and visit our website at sutherlandhousebooks.com for more information about our authors and their schedules.

Manufactured in Canada
Cover designed by Lena Yang
Book composed by Karl Hunt

Library and Archives Canada Cataloguing in Publication
Title: Smart, successful & abused : the unspoken problem of domestic violence and high-achieving women / Angela Mailis.
Other titles: Smart, successful and abused
Names: Mailis, Angela, author.
Description: Includes bibliographical references.
Identifiers: Canadiana 2019012864X | ISBN 9781999439576 (hardcover)
Subjects: LCSH: Abused women. | LCSH: Women in the professions. | LCSH: Spousal abuse. | LCSH: Family violence.
Classification: LCC HV6626 .M35 2019 |
DDC 362.82/92—dc23

ISBN 978-1-9994395-7-6

This book is dedicated to Dr. Elana Fric-Shamji,
whose tragic death was the single most
compelling reason for it to be written

CONTENTS

PREFACE

AWOKE EARLY ONE Saturday morning to find a message from a medical colleague on my cellphone: "Did you hear about Mo?" A CP24 news channel link was attached. I opened it and stared in shock. The previous day, Friday, December 2, 2016, the body of Dr. Elana Fric-Shamji, a Toronto family physician, had been found in a discarded suitcase. Her husband, Mo Shamji, a Toronto Western Hospital neurosurgeon, was charged with first-degree murder.

I screamed in disbelief, bringing my husband, Norm, running into the room. All I could say was "This is not possible!" I suddenly remembered that yesterday morning, the day Elana's body had been found, my younger son, Alex, a chiropractor at my Pain and Wellness Centre, had called me with a strange message. He had had to cancel his first appointment because a police investigation had closed his route to work. Now I understood why: Elana's body had been discovered close to my son's Kleinburg home and to my clinic in Vaughan, north of Toronto.

I did not know Elana Fric-Shamji but I knew her husband, Mo Shamji, very well. He had been a colleague and a collaborator at Toronto Western Hospital, where I had spent most of my professional life as founder and director of the Comprehensive Pain Program. The news of Elana's murder and the charge against Mo horrified me.

I was not alone. By 7:30 that morning, my phone started ringing with calls from stunned members of my former staff at Toronto

Western, as well as from patients whom Mo and I had shared. None of us could believe the news. None of us could fathom that the quiet, aloof man we thought we knew, this very talented neurosurgeon, could be capable of what the media was reporting.

The news shook me to the bone. For the next few nights, I would awaken over and over, thinking of what had happened. In the morning, I would devour newspapers and watch TV news, thirsty for information. CTV News reported, from a source close to the investigation, that Elana Fric-Shamji's family and friends were alleging that her twelve-year marriage had long been a violent relationship. In the spring of 2005, police had been called to the couple's home in Ottawa, where Mo was attending medical school. Mo was charged with one count of assault and two counts of uttering threats. Allegedly, he had thrown Elana down the stairs when she refused to have an abortion, causing her to flee with their baby daughter. A peace bond, forbidding Mo from approaching Elana, was imposed by the courts. It was removed within three months to allow Mo to travel abroad for more training, something he could not do if he had a criminal record.

Elana's friends and colleagues began to approach me directly because they knew I had worked closely with Mo for several years. At a medical conference, a physician told me that Elana had been one of her brightest colleagues, very intelligent, and with leadership ability; however, after she had met Mo, her career took second place. Everything was now about his career. My colleague went on to say that she and all of Elana's friends had expected "something bad was going to happen to Elana." But, she added, "never that bad." They used to call Mo "wacko" and he was known to be extremely controlling.

More chilling details emerged through the media about the life and death of this thirty-nine-year-old doctor and mother of three. The *Globe and Mail* reported on April 4, 2017, that Elana's parents,

Ana and Joseph Fric, had stated in civil proceedings that Dr. Shamji
had committed another "serious assault" on Elana two months before
her murder. This, along with Elana's knowledge of Mo's involvement
with another woman, had prompted her to file for divorce. A week
before her death, Elana's lawyer had sent Dr. Shamji a formal email
requesting details of his financial assets.

Dr. Elana Fric-Shamji's murder shook the whole University
Health Network—the largest such network in Canada, comprised
of five hospitals, including Toronto Western, where Mo and I had
worked. Besides being a well-respected family physician, beloved
of colleagues and patients, Elana had made her mark as a very
active member of the Ontario Medical Association. At a May 2017
Canadian Pain Society conference that I attended in Halifax, her
name came up often. I tried to find out if anyone (colleagues, nurses,
secretaries) had observed anything out of line in Mo's behavior. One
recalled an incident at a scientific conference, a year or so previously. During dinner in a posh restaurant, Mo had ordered a bottle
of wine, costing close to $250. When he didn't like it, he'd made a
loud scene, demanding that the wine be changed. According to this
colleague, the whole group was "looking at the floor throughout
the altercation," shocked by Mo's display of serious anger for such a
small thing. That had made no sense to anyone back then. Now, it
made total sense to all of us.

Other observations that had seemed insignificant took on sinister
shape and meaning. I was told that Mo occasionally appeared at
work with bruises that he attributed to hitting a door or slipping,
and so forth. In hindsight, these injuries suggested frequent alterca-
tions in which Elana had defended herself by hitting back. Most
shocking, apart from Elana's murder itself, was the fact that Mo had
gone to the hospital the next morning and operated all day, as if
nothing had happened. When nurses had commented on bruises to
his face, he had again downplayed them. I was also told that several

of his co-workers had had to take trauma counseling after Elana's murder, partly out of disbelief that Dr. Shamji was able to operate without any signs of emotional distress.

According to a 2015 Statistics Canada study,[1] almost 92,000 Canadians were victims of intimate partner violence, representing 28 percent of all victims of police-reported violent crime. Four out of five of these were women—about 72,000 females. Of the 964 intimate-partner homicides between 2005 and 2015, 74 percent were committed by a marital or common-law spouse.

In the United States, women account for 85 percent of victims of intimate partner violence. One in four women experience severe violence, bringing the total number of American women who are physically attacked by an intimate partner every year to 4,774,000. A woman in the United States is beaten every nine seconds and one in seven women has been injured by an intimate partner (the same proportion, incidentally, that have been stalked). Intimate partner violence accounts for 15 percent of all American violent crime. Three women are murdered every day by a current or former male partner. In 2011, 926 women were murdered by an intimate partner. Of those, 264 were killed during an argument. Intimate partner violence is the leading cause of female homicide[2] and injury-related deaths during pregnancy.[3]

Here is another way to look at it. The number of American troops killed in Afghanistan and Iraq between 2001 and 2012 was 6,488. The number of women murdered by current or former male partners during that time was 11,766, nearly double. And worldwide, 70 percent of women will experience physical and/or sexual abuse by an intimate partner during their lifetimes.

My connection to Elana felt deep and personal, aside from my professional connection to her husband. For twenty-seven years, I, too, had been involved in an emotionally (but not physically) abusive relationship. Elana's murder caused me to return with a sense of urgency to a book that I had been writing, on and off, for fifteen years. What initially had been a project intended to purge my emotional pain now acquired a sense of mission. I decided to concentrate on what outsiders would consider the most puzzling form of domestic abuse—the abuse endured over many years by high-achieving women like myself and Elana. How could we women—highly educated, confident professionals, entrepreneurs, powerhouses in the boardroom—allow ourselves to be mentally dominated and emotionally beaten down by our husbands? Why would we endure for years, for decades, such abusive behavior?

Those were questions I had been asking myself over many years. Once my difficult, protracted, and expensive divorce had receded into my rearview mirror, I started to gain some clarity about what I had endured. Even to me, it was incongruous that a woman with excellent skills in verbal communication, goal-setting, and financial competency would prove at such a loss in her private relationship. The confidence I exhibited in my professional milieu was forgotten, misplaced, or repressed as soon as I walked through the door of my own home. It was as though I turned into a different person: two selves, each on a parallel track but behaving in totally different manners.

Looking back from the security of a second, supportive marriage, I still shake my head in disbelief at my level of tolerance for mistreatment. *Smart, Successful, Abused* is the product of my long, painful, and frightening journey out of that pit. As I gained mental, physical, and emotional balance after my divorce, I started talking to other women whom I knew as friends and colleagues. To my initial surprise, I discovered that many were trapped in dangerous relationships that they were unwilling, or unable, to leave. Through my work as a pain doctor for more than three decades, I had also learned that my patients' crippling physical pain could sometimes be traced to emotional distress caused by domestic abuse.

It hit me hard to realize that Elana had been "one of us."

When I started this book, I was convinced that bringing my story and the stories of other women to public attention was a worthwhile goal. I sought professional answers and interpretations in the medical literature, expanded the circle of women whom I was interviewing, and created a forum at my home for discussion. Later, I designed an experimental survey to see how younger women, in dating relationships, were responding to emotional and physical male dominance.

Walking with others through this journey of mutual self-discovery has made me confident and secure enough to be able to take an objective look at my life and the lives of these other women, to call it as I see it—or as I should have seen it. Now I can dissect my bad relationship and identify the elements that made me (and so many others) vulnerable. I can also look critically at the process of awakening, at the steps to establishing a better life. Though all the high-achieving women that I introduce in this book lived dual lives, we took different routes from that starting point. Some of us went all the way to liberation, integrating our inner selves with our confident, strong, independent outer selves. Some never escaped dysfunctional environments. Still others fluctuated between freedom and subordination, leaving one bad relationship only to fall into another, always hoping that this will be the good one.

I start this book by writing about my upbringing in Greece. I highlight the independence that caused me to seek professional advancement in Canada, along with the insecurities that made me susceptible to emotional abuse, and the triggers that finally caused me to escape my twenty-seven-year entrapment. I examine the literature on these subjects, analyzing what constitutes physical, mental, and emotional abuse, paying special attention to successful career women. I provide a list of questions to help readers analyze their own relationships, and I explain "mirroring," a technique I found useful for integrating my inner and outer selves. From there, I relate stories of real women who suffered at the hands of their partners. This is the core of the book. I also describe the forum that I established for women with troubling relationships to compare notes and gain insights from each other.

In the latter half of the book, I explore the ten main reasons why high-achieving women are susceptible to abusive relationships, and why they stay in them. I back this up with more case histories. I look critically at high-achieving victims and the maladaptive mechanisms that contribute to our own suffering. I examine the flawed logic we use to rationalize our relationships – wobbly thinking we would never tolerate when making professional decisions. I describe the difficult process of realizing that such damaging relationships cannot be fixed, followed by the steps we face in escaping them. For me, returning to Greece for a reunion was a watershed in my journey of self-discovery. Other women I spoke with described their own defining moments.

Towards the end, I discuss the long and winding road from separation through the divorce courts, and describe the challenges of depleted finances and the impact of these changes on the kids, as well as the challenge of being single once again. Through personal anecdote, I relate the highs and lows of dating after bad relationships have left us bruised. I examine whether the boardroom's touted gender equality for intelligent and successful women has reached the bedroom.

Finally, I describe a small research project in which I question the attitudes, beliefs, and expectations of today's young, educated women, in regard to relationships. The results may stun you, as they did me. The epilogue reflects on my journey, and returns to the story of Elana Fric-Shamji.

I hope that my "coming out" will educate and empower other women, especially those leading double lives—who are successful in their careers but timid, hurt, and hiding at home. I hope that all domestically abused women will find support in knowing they are not alone. I also hope this book will prompt readers to open up and share their personal stories in forums and in book clubs. As I discovered, the support of other women can be a fundamental first step in healing. Perhaps most importantly, I hope this book will educate young women—our daughters, our nieces, our daughters-in-law and their friends—so that they can recognize and deflate the delusions that entrapped so many of us in the forties-to-sixties demographic. Partner abuse is, tragically, endemic to our culture. If this book ends up helping a few women, it will be worth the years and deep emotion I have invested in it. Maybe it will even help to prevent the untimely death of someone like Elana.

CHAPTER 1

One Life, Two Selves

I N SEPTEMBER 1986, at age thirty-four, I left the hospital with my second son, Alex. At two days old, he was a big, happy boy with only two thoughts in mind: hanging on to my breast and sleeping. My mother, who was visiting from Greece, had come with my husband, Johnny, to pick me up. They were seated in front while I was in the back with my precious bundle strapped beside me. Though I was tired, in some pain, and feeling a little down, I was looking forward to being home. My husband suddenly asked, "Do you have our house key?"

With my mind clouded by the eventful last two days, I replied, "I don't remember where I left it." He snapped back, "Where is your brain? This isn't the first time you've lost important stuff! That's what happens when you're too busy at work. You don't pay attention to what goes on at home." His tirade of complaints went on for the half-hour ride: my poor memory, my deficient housekeeping skills, my constant carelessness, and so forth. My mother was shocked speechless, afraid to intervene lest she provoke more insults. My eyes turned into taps. Given my postpartum condition, the front of my dress was soaked by the time we reached home.

I cannot count the number of similar incidents during my twenty-seven-year relationship with Johnny (seventeen of those years as a married couple). Whenever something minuscule upset him, the first thought that galloped into my head was oops, I screwed up again. I would apologize, then meekly sit through his barrage of insults and accusations, mistakenly believing that agreeing with his catalogue of my shortcomings would bring peace. The triggers for Johnny's outbursts were random and endless. He might be jealous of someone I'd talked with or angry about an innocent comment, or maybe he did not like the dinner I had prepared or how I had dealt with our sons.

He would lash out at me in any environment. During a short speech at a gala dance of the Greek Canadian Medical Association in the early 1990s, Johnny started talking loudly to one of my staff, whom I'd invited as a guest. I whispered to him, "Please don't talk now, everyone can hear you." He shouted even louder: "How dare you interrupt me?" Then he unleashed a cascade of insults about the attendees, the service, and the food. My clinic coordinator, a close friend, distracted Johnny by walking him out of the banquet hall for a smoke, leaving behind a pool of embarrassment and spoiling what had been an evening of good fun.

These outbursts were not the only problems troubling our marriage. Other issues connected to my work and to our intimacy caused endless contention. In fact, everything I did was criticized, always. As the years went by, I often wondered what the hell was wrong with me. I was a medical doctor with a national and international reputation who commanded respect from colleagues and staff. As the family's sole breadwinner, I made sound decisions about my career and household finances. I was one of those superwomen who always attended parent-teacher interviews, drove the kids to swimming classes, and organized movies and puppet shows on the weekend. Yet every time I opened the door to my house, I transformed into someone I could not recognize: a timid, insecure person who worried about "making things right" for my spouse's approval.

My self-questioning became insistent. What had turned me into this strangely conflicted, two-track person? I was born in 1952 in Neo Phaliron, a suburb of the famous Piraeus harbor, close to Athens. My sister, Pari, followed fifteen months later. Dad was from a part of southern Greece called Mani, an autocratic, male-dominated society where men always had the first and last word. He was a true patriarch, an honorable man with a strict work ethic, the eldest of six brothers and sisters who often sought his counsel. Despite his leadership role, he rarely spoke; he concealed his emotions and made few physical or verbal displays of affection.

My mother was one of eight siblings born to a wealthy family in Sparta in the Southern Peloponnese. When my grandfather, the assistant mayor of the town, died suddenly from septic shock due to an infected tooth, the family was plunged into poverty. Three of his children, including my mother, had to work to support the family. Johnny and I met in 1968, in my first year of senior high, when I was sixteen and Johnny was two years older. He was handsome, with thick, dark, wavy hair. Though a bit shorter than me, his build was sturdy and muscular from training with weights. He played the guitar well enough to be in amateur bands and he sang nicely the songs of the artists of our times—the Beatles, Simon & Garfunkel, Cat Stevens. On the other side of the ledger, he was a poor student who skipped most of his classes. He smoked cigarettes and pot, drank, and partied. He was a quintessential bad boy, chased by many girls. That gave me an inexplicable rush.

My reputation as our school's best student, yet hard to tame, was enticing to Johnny. I was loud, and mentally and physically hyperactive, with my boldness covering low self-esteem. I hated everything about my looks, particularly my unruly curly hair and my height—traits that, much later, I came to like. Back then, I felt I was too tall for a Greek girl. Though holding the flag in school parades was an honor reserved for the best student, it reinforced my sense of being a walking hydro pole. I was consumed by jealousy when I compared myself to girls with better bodies, long, straight hair, and big eyes, who had males in hot pursuit.

The fact that sexy Johnny was attracted to me seemed unbelievable. It offered the validation I was seeking. I felt myself falling deeply in love with him despite our differences in academic achievement, in temperament, and in family values. Johnny's father had been a minister's son, born on one of the Dodecanese islands in the Aegean Sea. Though he came to Athens to study dentistry, I believe he dropped out to marry Johnny's mother. He was a difficult man with a spotty work record. When the marriage broke up, due to constant friction, Johnny's younger sister went with their mother, while Johnny chose to remain with his father.

Johnny was my first and—I hoped—my last love. I was overwhelmed with my good luck in having captured the gem so many other girls wanted. From the start, Johnny was not easy. He was often late for our rendezvous in the half-hour before school, which was the only time I could steal from under my parents' watchful eyes. He was extremely jealous, which, in my naïveté, I interpreted as a manifestation of his great love. At the same time, I was petrified he would physically attack—yet again—any boy he perceived might be my potential suitor.

Johnny dropped out of high school to become a dental technician. He then spent two years in the army, as all able-bodied Greek males were obliged to do. Meanwhile, I was accepted into the University of Athens Medical School, which I attended from 1970 to 1976. While going to university, I lived at home, with Johnny mostly off in the army.

At medical school, my reputation as an aggressive devourer of books intimidated my classmates, especially when it came to oral exams. No one was happy to be grouped with me, because my presence raised the bar by making our questions harder. Nothing academic intimidated me, leading to my nicknames of "Holy Terror" and "Bulldozer." Apparently, my fondness for short, tight skirts resulted in another nickname—"Legs"—which I did not learn about until many years later.

When my parents discovered my relationship with Johnny, they were utterly opposed. I fought constant battles with my father, who objected to Johnny's poor education and careless values. He was terrified that I might become pregnant and abandon my studies. My father's hard stance and my mother's constant nagging only made me stubborn and unyielding. Many years after my divorce, my sister Pari said she was convinced that, if our parents had "just let me be," I would have realized my mistake and left Johnny on my own accord.

Instead, every few months, I would see him during his brief leaves from his military camp located far from Athens. He also phoned whenever he could get an evening's pass and find a phone booth. By then, I had lost contact with my high-school classmates and was so immersed in university studies and student politics that I had few friends. When popular male students approached me, I kept them at bay with a rather condescending facade. Looking back, I now believe that was my way of protecting myself from temptation, since I assumed I would marry Johnny.

My relationship with those in authority continued to be strained. What had begun as a clash with my father escalated into a clash with the government, the police, the university administration, my professors, and members of the student body when they considered their political agenda more important than education. After my final pharmacology exam in my second year of medicine, I offered to stay behind to collect the papers. As soon as the room had cleared, my supervisor began to make sexually aggressive remarks. My insistent rejection only fueled his desire, so that we ended up playing tag around the desks. With my heart pounding from anxiety, I abruptly stopped to confront him. Feet firmly planted, I warned: "You take one more step, and I'll level you to the ground!"

Since I towered over him, he retreated into verbal threats. "Then you will never pass this exam!"

That stoked my wrath. "You bastard! I am an A+ student, and I know I aced this paper. If you dare fail me, I swear to God, I'll pull your pants down to your knees in the middle of the university campus!"

That did it. I got my A, and we never again exchanged words.

I had another memorable clash with authority in 1974 after Greece's military junta was overturned by the democratically elected socialist party, causing exiled profs to reclaim their stolen academic chairs. By then, I had been elected to the student council as a member of the student socialist party. My platform had been the mobilization of students to improve our teaching facilities and to fight for students' rights.

Our twelve-member student government—three girls and nine boys—was a coalition of parties, ideologies, and personalities. My socialist party held four seats, three men and me. When female students complained to me that one of the returning professors was groping girls in his office and threatening to fail them if they resisted, I meticulously collected testimonials and then approached my male party members to bring this action to student council. All adamantly refused. Because the old groper was a staunch party supporter, they insisted the matter must be settled quietly, but without specifying how.

That blew my mind. To this day, I remember standing on campus loudly cursing my male peers for their self-serving toeing of the party line. Though my language had always been uninhibited, that day I sounded like a truck driver with road rage. I had joined the socialist party because I believed it would undo the junta's corrupt seven-year reign. This was just one more disillusioning event that peeled off my veneer of innocence and caused me to resign from student council.

I look back on my years at Athens Medical School as marked by sex, politics, and injustice. Yet, while I fought public wars against authority, I remained subservient to Johnny as my personal authority, giving in, reconciling, justifying his actions, coddling him. Even when my father, in an attempt to end our relationship, cut off financial support except for the roof over my head, I was unfazed. In my first year, I translated medical texts from English to Greek. I taught biology and chemistry in English to Middle Eastern students. In my second year, I also sold books door to door and subsequently created a book-selling team from whom I received commissions. While still at the head of my class, I was making the salary of a full-time bank clerk, with no rent and few groceries to buy.

By 1974, Johnny had finished his army service, and had moved back with his father. He periodically held minor jobs, while receiving financial help from me. Typically, he blamed his problems on someone or something else—his parents' separation, incompetent co-workers, arrogant employers. The list went on. Though I shared my academic successes with him, I never talked about other guys who seemed attracted to me or about my skirmishes with authority. Instead, I empathized with him about how unfairly life was treating him. Any thought of leaving our relationship was squelched by his threats of suicide and by my fear that I would never find anyone else to love me as much as I thought Johnny loved me. I clung to the hope that with my encouragement he would do well in life. My strongest reason for staying? I wanted to prove to my parents that they were wrong; I even imagined that they, too, would learn to appreciate Johnny.

By the time I graduated from Athens Medical School in 1976, I had laid down the two-track pattern that would govern my next couple of decades: me, financially independent and successful; me, subservient to a man who treated me with disdain and worse. Whenever my high-school classmates saw my sister, they would ask, "Is Angela still with Johnny?" My sister would nod yes and change the subject.

My university experience, coupled with what I saw as a lack of meritocracy in the Greek medical and political systems, convinced me that being an intelligent, ambitious, good-looking woman (whether or not I agreed with this opinion) was a recipe for failure in Greece. This fueled my desire to emigrate to North America for medical training. By then, I had helped Johnny financially to open his own pizza café in a wealthy suburb of Athens. Since he knew my drive for my studies was unstoppable, and since his pizza business was doing well, his "leash" on me had loosened. Our plan was for me to train abroad, with both of us exchanging visits as often as possible. After that, I was to return to Athens to set up a permanent medical practice.

I took the exams I needed to validate my Greek medical degree, and then applied to Canada and the United States for internships. By a twist of fate, the American government suddenly changed its qualifying criteria for foreign physicians so that I was eligible only in Canada. In the spring of 1978, I received my greatest gift ever—acceptance as a resident trainee at Mount Sinai Hospital in Toronto. I was to work in the physical medicine and rehabilitation unit, dealing with disabled patients, an offer I received only because no qualified Canadian was interested.

A month before my departure, after a troubled ten-year courtship, I married my high-school sweetheart. Johnny had rented a small basement apartment where we lived until I left for Canada. We had a quiet little ceremony in a Greek church with only fifteen people in attendance, including my sister and my aunt, and with my parents conspicuously absent. I was later told that my mother had to stay behind because my father "was going out of his mind" the day of the wedding. Both of them were convinced that the intellectual and emotional differences between Johnny and me were so vast that our marriage was surely headed for failure. All the same, my emigration meant I was putting my studies first, so my father gladly supported my departure.

On June 17, 1978, I arrived in Toronto, excited to pursue my dream but with a heavy heart at leaving behind the man I dearly loved, along with my family. I rented a furnished bachelor apartment close to the hospital, and started the greatest adventure of my life. I was all alone, throwing myself into a new country, a new culture, a new language, a new medical environment. Though my formal English was excellent, thanks to years of translating texts on internal medicine, I was completely unprepared for Canadian slang, for other immigrants' broken English, and for the slurred speech of stroke patients. Spoken English proved an unexpected daily struggle. I remember being deeply offended when a patient called me a "smart cookie." I understood the word "smart," but "cookie"? That sounded like an insult until a smiling colleague explained its idiomatic meaning.

In those years, cultural sensitivity was nonexistent. Many of my hospital instructors were rude, demeaning, and offensive. Though most, like me, were foreign-born, they were perhaps passing on what they had experienced themselves. One exception was a young Jewish doctor, Perry, who was soft-spoken and intelligent with excellent teaching skills and, above all, a professional and moral compass similar to mine. In the early years of my training, he kindled my interest in chronic pain medicine. Years later, once we were both in practice, we spoke often and shared ideas and experiences of navigating the difficult political environment in our hospitals. Perry and I remain friends and collaborators.

By contrast, a few of my professors ridiculed my Greek accent, as did some uncouth patients. I was from outside of the white

Anglo-Saxon box. Nevertheless, I always asked my professors for explanations to make sure I understood, and I often challenged them. Mostly I had a good point, though I often caused offense by my lack of political correctness and my misunderstanding of the polished manner in which Canadians subtly conceal their exact meaning.

I was not an easy student. And the isolation and coldness of my social environment was overwhelming for a Greek woman who was used to large family gatherings and a vibrant culture. Returning late to an empty apartment in a cold city sent me spiraling into despair. Even my belief in my intellectual capacities began to crumble, to the point that I considered leaving. I lost a good ten to fifteen pounds in my first few months. I longed for my husband, and spent three-quarters of my tiny salary on long-distance phone calls. I also had biweekly communications with my parents and sister, hiding from them any knowledge of my struggles.

Instead of opening up to my family, I would talk out my troubles to my reflection in the square mirror that hung in my apartment's living room. Staring at the woman in that mirror, with black circles under her hooded eyes, with unmanageable curly hair, her cheeks streaming with tears, I repeated the same sentences over and over. *I do not want your doors. I do not want your windows. I just need a hole in the wall, the size of my little finger, and I will make it through.* After a year, my understanding of spoken English dramatically improved, my confidence returned, and my marks were back up in the top 5 percent of all residents in my specialty.

On a more personal note, my father softened up enough to meet with Johnny a few times, which seemed to me almost a miracle. My joy was short-lived, however. I had only been in Canada a few months when he was diagnosed with lung cancer. He was a heavy smoker. I returned to Greece in the summer of 1979, just after he had had part of his lung surgically removed. Tragically, his tumor grew back. My beloved father died suddenly in July 1980.

That summer, a toxic smog had hung over Athens, speeding his demise. After my father's funeral, I cut the umbilical cord tying me to my homeland. By then, Johnny's pizza business had begun to fail and he joined me in Toronto. After a while, we mutually decided to convert our visitors' visas to allow us to become permanent Canadian residents, a difficult and expensive process. In 1982, following a day trip to Buffalo, we finally and formally re-entered Canada as permanent residents.

Johnny was never happy in his new country. He longed for Greece's warmer climate, his friends and his parties, and soon became very depressed. In 1982, after he had traveled back and forth a few times, we bought our first little house, and he grew excited about renovating it. Then, while Johnny struggled with a variety of jobs, my career rapidly evolved so that I became our primary, then our sole, breadwinner.

In 1982, I obtained specialty certification in Physical Medicine and Rehabilitation from the Royal College of Physicians. That same year, I joined Toronto Western Hospital, where I founded the pain program that I would direct for more than thirty-three years. I obtained my master's degree from the Institute of Medical Science at the University of Toronto and in 2005 became a full professor in the Faculty of Medicine. In 2014, I created my new Pain and Wellness Centre in Vaughan, the only community-based academic pain program funded by the Ontario Ministry of Health. While my clinical and research work established my national and international reputation, my popular writings about chronic pain attracted many lay readers. Today, regulatory bodies, pharmaceutical companies, legal firms, and government bodies continue to seek my expertise. I have published many papers in several scientific journals. I have lectured around the world, and I have been the subject of multiple features in print and on television.

Over the forty years I have lived in Canada, I did make it through that hole in the wall that I so fervently wished for. Escaping my marriage, however, would be a fraught process. As a scientist, I have always taken pride in asking questions, expecting that sooner or later I will find the answers. Even with my pragmatic temperament, it took me years to realize that I had split myself into a professional go-getter and an insecure, giving, and forgiving pleaser.

My first son, Nicholas, was born in April 1985, almost six weeks prematurely, while I was in the lab working on my master's thesis. My second, Alex, was born in September 1986, as I've described. The boys were the light of my life. I thought Johnny was a good father, although my sons now tell me they have some not-so-happy memories of him. His work record continued to be spotty, yet I still had to employ nannies to help me with the kids. I continued to be the person who attended teacher-parent interviews, who helped the boys with their schoolwork, who drove them to piano lessons, to soccer, to swimming, to the theater, to Muppet shows. I also participated on school boards, and helped to create the first Greek language school in East York, where we lived for many years. I did this the grassroots way, by collecting door-to-door signatures and then canvassing the Ministry of Education.

My busyness helped me to hide, even from myself, the misery of my life with a dependent, demeaning, and destructive husband. For years, I navigated my contradictory roles—the professional self who commanded respect from co-workers and colleagues, and my miserable personal self. To hide my shame, I created a mask. I distorted the truth by praising my husband loudly for little things that were not worth the praise, and by lying to family and friends about his job (that is, the fact he did not have one). I pretended so hard that I became the primary victim of my own manufactured truth.

The preparatory period, leading to my liberation, started a few months before my fortieth birthday. Years of sedentary, sixty-hour workweeks had physically deconditioned me. Meanwhile, Johnny had become a six-pack exercise freak with a fully equipped basement gym. Puffed with pride, he constantly goaded me about my looks. "Your boobs are sagging. Your butt is hanging." With these insults engraved on my brain, I told myself I could either spiral down into a deep, dark hole, or let his words piss me off enough to react. I went for that second choice.

With anger now a driving force, I asked my husband to order a home-based fitness machine so I could exercise in the house instead of going to a gym. Early in 1992, a NordicTrack stationary skiing machine, guaranteed to provide a total-body workout, arrived at our home. Johnny set it up in one of the kids' bedrooms, and that same night I climbed aboard. My balance on the skis was terrible. I slipped off every couple of minutes while Johnny stood in the doorway, taunting me. "You see? You can't even do this. I'll return it."

That was exactly the push I needed. Overwhelmed by rage, supported by long, slow-burning resentment, I stubbornly climbed onto that damned machine every night while my younger son tried to sleep against the rhythmical sound of the sliding skis. It took only a week for me to learn. After a couple more weeks, I was doing daily half-hour workouts and raising my resistance, preparing me for increased time on the machine. Soon, the rewards started to appear.

In three months, I went down two dress sizes. In six months, my resting heart rate went down from the seventy-six-to-seventy-eight beats per minute range to sixty-two-to-sixty-four beats, a sign of cardiovascular conditioning. I was exhilarated, especially when my staff and others began complimenting me. For the first time in my life, I started liking me. I had taken the time to care about my reflection, the external one in the mirror and the internal one in my mind's eye.

I pursued more fitness avenues. I fell in love with aerobic line dancing. When I started taking two-hour dance classes twice a week, Johnny grudgingly agreed to look after the kids, believing this to be a fad that would pass. The more fit I became, the more at ease I grew about my looks, leading to a change in the way I dressed.

As a teenager, and even at university, I had found high heels too wobbly to wear. Dancing tremendously improved my balance and coordination so that I soon mastered 2½- to 3-inch heels. No more worries about my height. While I had spent my teenage years trying to straighten my curly hair, now I liked it natural, with every tendril stretching past my shoulders. I also consulted a professional makeup artist and then found a one-stop boutique where the owner matched designer dresses with accessories. Within an hour, I would go home with four or five elegant outfits.

As my confidence in my physical self skyrocketed, my emerging inner self's confidence began to match it. My final wakeup call came, literally, at 3 a.m. in May 1993. My brother-in-law, Koulis, was calling from Greece with chilling news. "Pari was diagnosed with severe anemia, and the doctors are afraid it's a symptom of something bad."

My sister Pari, at thirty-nine, was a regular blood donor. Despite unusual fatigue, she had gone to her clinic to donate. That is when the staff had discovered her low blood-cell count. Koulis was distraught. Not trusting local health care, he phoned me to discuss bringing Pari to Toronto, where I could provide her with resources for diagnosis and treatment. I immediately made the arrangements with my hospital colleagues.

A week later, I picked Pari up from the airport and took her to an appointment with a well-known hematologist, a specialist who deals with diseases of the blood. Within a week, all of Pari's blood work was completed, including a biopsy of her bone marrow, which is the soft, paste-like tissue inside bones that serves as a factory for producing different types of blood cells. My worst fears were confirmed. My dear little sister, the mother of two daughters, then sixteen and fourteen, a woman who had always exuded an energetic embrace of life, who loved to travel and to dance, had multiple myeloma, a form of bone cancer. It had developed from the uncontrollable growth of plasma cells, displacing normal blood cells in Pari's bone marrow. That this had happened at such a young age was a very bad sign. The prognosis? Death in just a few years.

When Pari's disease failed to respond to medication, I had myself tested as a potential donor for a bone marrow transplant. Unfortunately, I was not a genetic match. The only alternative was a then-experimental procedure called bone marrow auto-transplantation, reserved for terminal cases. Stem cells (a form of primitive cells with the capacity to morph into all kinds of other cells) would be harvested from Pari's blood. Then, after she had undergone intense chemotherapy to kill off the diseased bone marrow, her stem cells would be returned to her body to replace the malignant ones.

Pari went through several rounds of chemotherapy, and one of heavy radiation therapy, before her stored stem cells were infused back into her body. During four horrendous weeks, she suffered painful mouth ulcers and required hospitalization once again, this time in the Intensive Care Unit, for a blood clot that had formed in a big vein in her arm.

Throughout the months of Pari's treatments, I had horrifying anxiety spells, waiting for something to go wrong, as it so often did. Many times, between patient appointments, I would go to my office bathroom to cry my eyes out. I refused to listen to my favorite music station while driving to and from work. I refused to go to the gym. I was ridden by anger, fear, and immense sorrow at being unable to take away my sister's pain. I kept asking: Why is this nasty disease happening to my sweet little Pari?

Toronto Western Hospital, where I had my office, belongs to the same network as Toronto General, where Pari was hospitalized. Whenever I learned that something adverse was happening to her, I would cancel all my appointments so I could go to her bedside. One such episode involved a pneumothorax, meaning that blood had accumulated around Pari's lung. Despite all my medical training,

I fainted as I watched the surgical team insert a tube to drain her chest. My sister's overwhelming pain, combined with my feeling of impotence, had lowered my blood pressure sufficiently to drop me to the floor.

It ended with good news: Pari made it. Her infused bone marrow "took." After six months of treatment and a quarter of a million dollars paid through private insurance, she was able to return to Greece. Today, twenty-five years later, Pari is still enjoying her family, including her two granddaughters. The only downside is that she has developed severe arthritis as a result of the intense therapy she had at the time of auto-transplantation.

The six months Pari spent with me changed my life. Pari had been the second person in our family to receive a multiple myeloma diagnosis. My mother's sister had also developed this disease, though not until she was in her seventies. Their diagnoses meant that I, too, was genetically predisposed to this type of blood cancer. I was deeply shaken. My mortality hit me like a kick in the gut.

I realized, all of a sudden, that on my way to my grave, I was not going to regret the research paper I had not finished or the lecture I had not given. What I would mourn was my unlived life, the trips I had never taken, the sunsets I had not noticed, and—so much more important—the true, sustaining love I had always longed for. I questioned my whole outlook on life, tortured by all the years that had already slipped through my fingers.

These troubling thoughts were exacerbated by Johnny's despicable behavior throughout Pari's visit. He tortured me with complaints about his loss of privacy because he thought my dying sister was outstaying her welcome. Why, he insisted, could I not at least set a date for her return to Greece? Johnny's questions aroused some deeply buried questions of my own: How could I, at age forty-one, still be yoked to such a callous, selfish partner, and where the hell was I going with the rest of my life?

After Pari's return to Greece, I fell into a serious depression. I cried alone at the office and stayed late to avoid facing my own stark reality. My first step toward healing was to become aware that the way I lived my life was wrong and that the dysfunction was not all my fault. The next step was to ask myself some important questions about my past and my present, and then to act upon the answers for my future. Eventually, I accepted the fact that divorce was my only gateway to freedom. It would be the catalyst for the kind of life I wanted, and that I now believed I deserved, although I was still haunted by the prospect of wreaking havoc on my children's lives.

In the summer of 1995, I finally found the courage to leave my marriage. This was followed by a terrible year of police visits, mediations, court hearings, and expensive lawyers. My acrimonious divorce actually became known in Ontario's Family Court as one of the worse in the last thirty years, but I weathered that storm well. Not only did I make it, but my love for fitness after my divorce took me to martial arts for thirteen years, earning me a black belt in Tae Kwon Do. Later, I would buy a Harley Davidson motorcycle (my steel horse that I cherish on the open road to this day).

CHAPTER 2

Are You Caught in the Grip of Abuse?

RELATIONSHIPS DO NOT TURN sour overnight. We are conditioned during long periods of time to gradually accept and adapt to them, eventually losing sight of what is right or wrong and who we really are. In my dark years, I confided only in my longtime friend and secretary, Anna. In my willful state of denial, I assumed the outside world, including my neighbors, friends, and colleagues, believed I was happily married. After I initiated my divorce in July 1995, I was surprised to learn that my team members had been betting for years on how long my tumultuous marriage would last.

At the staff parties that were held twice a year at my home, the disconnect between Johnny and me had been especially obvious. My greatest concern, while I singlehandedly looked after our guests, was whom Johnny was going to offend. On one occasion, he went into a tirade against "men who paint their hair." It was clear that he was ridiculing one of the doctors on my team who used hair dye. At a potluck Christmas party, hosted by one of my staff members, Johnny spent the evening in a sulk, refusing to speak to me, deliberately sitting as far away as possible, and neglecting to help me with the boys, who were still quite young. Though my staff could see he was angry, only I knew the reason. On the way to the party, for which I had cooked a pan of moussaka, Johnny had exploded: "Why do you cook so much food for strangers, instead of for your family?"

Despite all of these signs, no one on my staff had tried to offer me marital advice because they knew I was stubborn and not yet ready to admit to defeat. I was clueless. Even when I walked out of my marriage, I did not understand what specifically was wrong with it and why I had been willing to accept such a bad deal. That ended when Anna gave me *The Verbally Abusive Relationship: How to Recognize It and How to Respond*, a 1992 book by Patricia Evans. In it, I found a list of seven questions used to determine if abuse is taking place. If you answered yes to two of them, you were declared to be a victim of verbal and emotional abuse. I answered yes to five. What a revelation. I ran out of my office, yelling, "Can you believe it, Anna? I just found out that I've been verbally and emotionally abused all these years!" Could I blame Anna for rolling her eyes?

I believe that abuse is at the core of most bad relationships. As the Center for Relationship Abuse Awareness puts it, abuse is a pattern of coercive behaviors used to maintain power and control over a former or current intimate partner. Abuse may occur in the workplace, in educational institutions, in sports or recreational organizations, or in religious environments. But most often it is found in the home, where it is defined as domestic abuse.

A broad consensus maintains that women are subject to abuse significantly more than men. Abuse can be physical, emotional, sexual, spiritual, or a combination of these. Because physical abuse leaves physical evidence, it has been the subject of intense research in both scientific publications and the popular media, with significant societal repercussions for abusers. However, emotional abuse has been remarkably neglected. While it is much easier to hide, it is just as harmful. Its victims bury it in silence because of shame, and because they, like me, may not understand what is happening. Even after gaining insight, we may hesitate to name emotional abuse, because an emotionally abused woman has only one legal recourse: separation and divorce.

James O'Neil, a professor of Educational Psychology and Family Studies Psychology at the University of Connecticut, defines emotional abuse as "abuse that includes verbal expressions and behaviors that undermine a person's sense of self."[4] Similarly, Joan Lachkar, a distinguished California marriage and family therapist, defines it as "one partner's attempts to damage and destroy psychologically the will, the needs, the desires, or the perceptions of the other partner, either consciously or unconsciously."[5]

Emotional abuse frequently precedes and/or coexists with physical abuse. Lachkar points out that, while physical abuse occurs cyclically and intermittently, emotional abuse is usually chronic, happening all or most of the time. Its distinctive characteristic is its creeping, insidious nature. It eats its victim, one nibble at a time. An abuser's tactics include ridicule, shame, blame, criticism, threats, and neglect of their partner's emotional needs.

Emotional abuse may be overt (obvious to everyone) or covert (hidden).[6] Overt abuse takes the form of public putdowns, criticism, and name-calling. Although covert abuse is subtle, it is equally devastating and demeaning. In the 1944 movie *Gaslight*, a husband (Charles Boyer) attempts to convince his wife (Ingrid Bergman) that she is going insane by constantly denying her version of reality. When he causes the lights in their Victorian-era home to dim and then to brighten, he insists this is not happening, persuading his wife that she must be delusional. So effective was this spooky device that the term "gaslighting" is now often used in the psychological literature to describe emotional abuse. So subtle. So constant. So mind-numbing.

Years after Lachkar's seminal 1998 book, *The Many Faces of Abuse: Treating the Emotional Abuse of High-Functioning Women*, Evan Stark of Rutgers University–Newark added to our understanding of the many forms of domestic abuse with his 2009 book *Coercive Control: How Men Entrap Women in Personal Life*. Stark's concepts are helpful in understanding why emotional abuse has become more prevalent in the home. He defines coercive control as "an ongoing pattern of domination by which male abusive partners primarily interweave repeated physical and sexual violence with intimidation, sexual degradation, isolation and control. The primary outcome of coercive control is a condition of entrapment that can be hostage-like in the harms it inflicts on dignity, liberty, autonomy and personhood as well as to physical and psychological integrity."

Stark points out that the recent recognition of domestic violence in the Western world as a serious problem and a criminal offense has had an enormous impact on courts, health care, child welfare, academia, and other facets of life. However, the equation of abuse with physical force in relationships has failed victimized women in serious ways. One of these is a failure to recognize that emotional abuse and coercive control involving minor violence, or no violence, is nevertheless enormously detrimental to victims.

I agree with Stark that coercive control is a relatively modern phenomenon, one that "men have devised . . . to offset the erosion of sex-based privilege in the face of women's gains." In cultures where law, custom, and traditions legitimize male domination, coercive control is not necessary. In Western societies like ours, where equality is formally endorsed and applied in our workplaces and our social and political environments, men are driven to "recreate their superiority and privilege in personal life." Stark also stresses that when one immigrates from a culture that endorses subordination to a society promoting equality, coercive control becomes stronger. He urges cross-cultural research to explore these issues.

The law has not kept up with our improved understanding of domestic abuse. Few countries include psychological or emotional abuse in their definitions of domestic violence, although there are a few exceptions. France has a separate criminal statute prohibiting psychological abuse and the parliament of the Republic of South Africa included emotional abuse in its definition of domestic violence. In 2012, England expanded its cross-governmental definition of domestic violence to encompass coercive control, and in 2015 coercive control became a new offense under U.K. law.

The urgency of these problems is borne out by the numbers. One in three American women have experienced at least one form of intimate partner violence in their lifetime, whether physical violence, rape, or stalking. Forty-eight percent have experienced psychologically aggressive behavior by an intimate partner.[7] What's more, virtually all women who report physical abuse at the hands of their partners also report psychological abuse.

The human rights agency Peace at Home has compiled a list of warning signs of emotional and physical abuse in an effort to educate the public.[8] Victims may experience several signs simultaneously.

Physical Abuse

1. Intimidation: Making angry or threatening gestures toward you; using greater physical size to intimidate you; standing in a doorway during arguments, as if to block your escape; shouting; driving recklessly.
2. Destruction: Destroying your possessions; punching walls; throwing and/or breaking items.
3. Threats: Making verbal threats to hurt you or others.
4. Sexual violence: Degrading treatment based on your gender or

sexual orientation; using coercion to obtain sex and the performance of sexual acts.

5. Physical violence: Being violent to you, your children, household pets, or others; slapping, punching, grabbing, kicking, choking, pushing, biting, etc.

6. Weapons: Possessing, displaying, or using weapons to frighten you.

Emotional Abuse

1. Verbal abuse: Name-calling, mocking, accusing, blaming, yelling, swearing; making humiliating remarks or gestures.

2. Pressure tactics: Using guilt-tripping and other forms of intimidation to rush you into making decisions unfavorable to yourself; sulking; manipulating the children; issuing orders.

3. Abusing authority: Always claiming to be right; insisting declarations are "the truth"; making decisions without consulting you; using false logic against you.

4. Disrespect: Interrupting; changing topics; not listening or responding; twisting your words; putting you down in front of others; insulting your friends and family.

5. Abusing trust: Lying; withholding information; cheating on you; being overly jealous.

6. Breaking promises: Not following through on agreements; failing to accept a fair share of responsibility; refusing to help with childcare or housework.

7. Emotional withholding: Not expressing feelings; denying you support, attention, or compliments; not respecting your feelings, rights, or opinions.

8. Minimizing, denying, and blaming: Making light of their own behavior while refusing to take your concerns seriously;

claiming the abuse did not happen; shifting responsibility for abusive behavior to you by insisting you caused it.

9. Economic control: Interfering with your work or not letting you work; withholding money or threatening to do so; taking your money; confiscating your car keys or otherwise preventing you from using the car; threatening to report you to welfare, or other social agencies, for imagined failings.

10. Self-destructive behavior: Abusing drugs or alcohol; threatening suicide or other forms of self-harm as an act of control; deliberately saying or doing things that have negative consequences (e.g., badmouthing you to your boss, spreading false rumors about your private life).

11. Isolation: Preventing or making it difficult for you to see friends and relatives; monitoring your phone calls; dictating where you can and cannot go.

12. Harassment: Making unwanted visits or calls to you; following you; checking up on you; embarrassing you in public; refusing to leave when asked.

The High-Functioning Woman

In 2017, Neha Rastogi, a thirty-six-year-old high-ranking Apple executive who worked closely with Steve Jobs on Siri and FaceTime, used her iPhone to record horrific domestic abuse perpetrated by her husband, another Silicon Valley luminary. He had assaulted her numerous times over their ten-year marriage, beating her when she was eight months pregnant and making her stand for the whole night afterwards, and slapping her for not breastfeeding their six-day-old child properly. He had once been taken into custody for assault after a mail carrier saw him punch his wife with a closed fist, but she bailed him out, thinking it best to keep her family together. The six-minute video she recorded when she had finally had enough including repeated thwacks heard in the presence of their then two-year-old daughter. It went viral on the internet. Her husband received ten days in jail.

It is a common misconception that domestic abuse is mostly confined to economically dependent, less educated women. In fact, abuse transcends culture, income, race, occupation and age, and it may, in fact, be that successful females are more vulnerable to abuse. Data from the U.S.-based National Coalition Against Domestic Violence show that women who earn 65 percent or more of their household's income are more likely to be psychologically abused than women who earn less. That suggests a widespread problem, given that women earn more than men in almost a quarter of opposite-sex couples. There is also plenty of anecdotal evidence that no amount of wealth and success can insulate women from abuse. Think of the well-publicized troubles of entertainers such as Tina Turner, Rihanna, and Robin Givens, all of whom have admitted to suffering domestic violence. The phenomenon of a smart, successful woman trapped in an abusive relationship was also central to the acclaimed HBO series *Big Little Lies*, based on the novel by Liane Moriarty. Nicole Kidman's character, Celeste, rewrites and erases her own history to keep up the false front of a perfect marriage.[9]

Joan Lachkar, in *The Many Faces of Abuse*, coined the phrase "high-functioning women."[10] That term applies to me and to the other women whose stories I will share. High-functioning women are well-educated, successful, and career oriented. They may be doctors, judges, lawyers, nurses, teachers, psychologists, entrepreneurs, executives. Though well respected in their professional and corporate worlds, many cannot replicate this success in their private lives. They learn to operate on two separate tracks. In their professional environment, they work cooperatively and lead teams. At home, their "victimized self" functions. Lachkar describes them as living a "conflicted, multilayered existence." Since many successful females marry equally successful mates, it is relevant to note that one-third of men counseled in emergency departments for battering their partners are professionals—doctors, psychologists, lawyers, ministers, business executives.[11]

Lachkar notes that society shows little understanding and tolerance for the emotionally abused woman. In fact, she is often scolded for putting up with her maltreatment. This attitude is particularly strong in the case of high-functioning women, who are viewed as privileged, with well-paying jobs and busy social lives. Often they dress expensively, take care of their appearance, and enjoy a prosperous lifestyle. While suppressing the truth about their abusive relationships, they present a facade designed to maintain their public status.

Unfortunately, behind this false self, these women are timid, vulnerable, and fragile, with numerous unmet personal needs. When women generally stayed home to raise children, they were targeted by abusive men for their perceived weakness and inferiority because they did not participate in the workforce. Now that more women are financially autonomous, they are targeted by male aggressors for these accomplishments. My awareness of this shift caused me to wonder if abuse, particularly the emotional kind, has increased since women began breaking the glass ceiling in the 1960s. The women's movement, coupled with economic growth in the developed world, has caused Western societies to become more focused on material goods and the status that success can buy. While many women have conspicuously improved their financial circumstances, many men have seen losses of steady, well-paid jobs. This fear of social change favoring women was often cited as a conspicuous factor in the anti-female fury directed against Hillary Clinton in the 2016 U.S. presidential elections.

"Superwoman syndrome" is an expression now widely used to refer to women who strive to excel in all aspects of life. A superwoman feels she must manage multiple roles, as a mother, as a caretaker to aging parents, as a career achiever. Unfortunately, such demands often result in the sacrifice of her own personal needs. Exhaustion, and fear of failure, may cause her to put up with an abusive husband, rather than admit she is not in control of this aspect of her life.

In *The Many Faces of Abuse*, Lachkar divides high-functioning women into two categories. One swings like a pendulum between a state of independence, authority, and control to a state of helplessness, guilt, despair, depression, and anxiety. Such women are ashamed to admit to emotional abuse because they fear, rightly, that this admission would lead to ridicule and disbelief. Lachkar believes these women accept abusive situations because of compelling psychosocial factors, such as a desire to preserve their marital bond, to keep their family together for the children, and to obey cultural tradition.

The other type of high-functioning woman remains self-deprecating and ridden by strong denial, shame, guilt, or blame. Such women beat up on themselves, believing everything is their fault. They also comfort themselves with magical thinking: they convince themselves that if only they hang in long enough, everything will somehow resolve itself.

Factors Leading to Acceptance of Abuse

Today Western societies have many more high-achieving women than they did four or five decades ago. What, in this context, breeds the vulnerability that leads to the abusive entrapment of so many of us? Experts agree on one central point. Some sort of deficiency existed in these women's early upbringing.

Psychologist D.W. Winnicott believes that, early in life, the high-functioning woman developed a false self in order to defend, insulate, and protect her true self, which was hurt or neglected by parents or other early caregivers.[12] While this seemingly confident false self took over her external world, her true self remained needy, deprived, hurt, and vulnerable. This caused her to be attracted to the kind of person who might seem to fulfill her unmet needs, but who, in reality, leads to a replication of the rejection, neglect, or abuse she experienced in her past.

While Lachkar also believes the building blocks for future emotional abuse were laid down at an early age, she is not prepared to accept that all high-functioning women have experienced serious childhood trauma or deprivation. She posits that any woman could get caught in the web of emotional abuse under certain circumstances. Based on my own experience, and that of the many other abused women I have encountered, I agree with Lachkar.

One of the patterns Lachkar cites as potentially leading to an acceptance of adult abuse occurs when a young person is forced to grow up too soon because of family circumstances, such as looking after a sick or disabled parent. I have firsthand experience of this pattern in my own family, and of its lasting detrimental effects. My mother was fourteen when her father died, leaving her as the sole caretaker of her mother, who had disabling Parkinson's disease. My mother was thirty-two when her mother died, which delayed her marrying and having children. As far back as I can remember, she reminded my sister and me of her sacrifice as a good daughter. She would constantly report her resentment over her lost youth and the lack of help from her siblings. I am not sure, however, if my father's totally domineering behavior constituted abuse, since Old World societies were traditionally more autocratic. "Do as I say," was the norm in regard to both women and children.

Just as dating sites offer compatibility based on personality types, Lachkar describes abusive relationships based on interlocking patterns. One common pair she describes is that of a narcissistic abuser uniting with a borderline woman. In psychoanalytical terms, a narcissistic abuser is dangerously self-absorbed and egotistical. "He is in love only with himself and often takes advantage of others." Very often, a narcissistic abuser was his mother's only or favorite child until a newborn sibling created feelings of neglect over his replacement. He often pairs with a needy, clingy woman, who experienced emotional starvation at an early age, causing her to become dependent. Though a borderline woman is excessively caring, giving, and kind, she may develop an unhealthy obsession to her partner, causing her to flip into someone aggressively dangerous to herself and others.

In the film *Fatal Attraction*, a married man (Michael Douglas) has a weekend affair with a successful editor of a publishing company (Glenn Close). Though it was supposed to be a one-time fling, the editor refuses to let go. In an attempt to entrap her lover, she slashes her wrists, stalks him, pretends to be pregnant, pours acid on his car, kills his daughter's pet rabbit, and then kidnaps his daughter. In a final dramatic scene, she is killed by her lover's wife.

The fact that this was 1987's highest-grossing film worldwide reflects both a recognition and a fascination with this pattern. Typical of Hollywood, *Fatal Attraction* hit every hot button in a narcissistic/borderline relationship. My colleague Jemma, an occupational therapist, and her husband, Philip, owner of a successful software company, are a more realistic example.

This couple, both multigenerational Canadians, lived in an upscale neighborhood in central Toronto. The only child of a well-heeled family, Philip spent most of his time and money on luxury cars, playing golf, and trips with "the boys." Jemma, the eldest of four sisters in a Maritimes family, had for many years taken care of her seriously ill mother and her siblings. As Philip's wife, Jemma spent most of her off-work hours caring for their two kids, helping them with their homework, and taking them to school and to after-school activities. Jemma often complained to me, in her soft-spoken way, about her husband's indifference to the children and his lack of support for her emotional and aspirational needs. When Jemma decided to return to university, Philip forced her to use money from her meager scholarship to hire a nanny. His narcissistic love for himself also made him callous and demeaning in his public treatment of Jemma—something I witnessed on a couple of social occasions.

Why did Jemma put up with this treatment for two decades? Having shouldered adult responsibilities at an early age, she had unmet emotional needs, turning her into the needy, clingy borderline woman that Lachkar describes.

As an example of another unhealthy coupling, Lachkar switches genders: a needy borderline male unable to bond because of early abandonment or emotional abuse, paired with a narcissistic woman in love with herself and unprepared or unable to fill his dependency needs. In Lachkar's experience, the borderline male, furious at the lack of nurturing available to him, is most likely to flip into aggression—like the editor in *Fatal Attraction*—to become a physical and emotional abuser. Unable to distinguish between his internal perceptions and his real environment, he makes poor partner choices and then forms a "parasitic bond." He often turns against himself before lashing out at others.

I asked my friend Tony Hunt, a psychologist whom I had consulted after my marital breakdown, why he thought women like me accept lives of abuse. Tony believes that we women, as young children, lacked true or perceived unconditional love. To compensate, we channeled our energies into work, earning conditional love based on our achievements. The professional environment then became an abuse-free place where we could advance our careers and utilize our assertiveness. When we came home, we turned to our partners for tenderness and intimacy to fill our empty void, expecting our needs to be met. Maybe we felt our professional skills of negotiation and self-assertion were not required here because we had falsely assumed love in marriage would be reciprocally unconditional. Instead, we were shunned, leaving us feeling even more vulnerable, hurt, and upset, and reinforcing our childhood confusion about who we really are.

Tony also suggested that financially independent, successful professional women like me might feel, deep in our hearts, that these qualities were "unfeminine," and that this was why we checked our professional skills at the door.

In my painful journey, while trying to reconcile my issues within myself and to learn to appreciate who I was, Tony taught me the profoundly helpful concept of mirroring. He encouraged me to view in a mirror my healthy, active, and successful self after I had embraced fitness as an integral part of my life, and then internalizing this same image in my mind's eye. The eyes of my friends and classmates later served as another mirror that I learned to internalize, allowing me to see myself as positively as they did. This helped me to integrate my two selves.

I hope this book will also serve as a mirror, allowing readers to see and to better understand themselves through the stories of abused women that they will encounter here. I hope it will help those of you living on parallel tracks to bridge your professional and personal worlds, enabling you to begin to extricate yourselves from abusive relationships.

Lachkar writes: "No woman deserves to be abused physically, sexually, or emotionally, and no one deserves to be undermined, mistreated, or violated. While women, including high-functioning women, are not responsible for the abuse, they are not helpless victims either." I agree. Yes, it takes time to understand that we have fallen into a bad relationship, great courage to get out of it, and serious effort to rebuild our lives, but it can be done—as evidenced by many of the women you will meet here. Everyone has the capacity to end victimization, and it is our responsibility to do all that is necessary to free ourselves.

CHAPTER 3

You Are Not Alone

ONCE I HAD LIBERATED myself and joined the ranks of the single, I became comfortable about opening up to talk about my past with other women. As I did, I was amazed to learn that my story was not unique. Many women, just like me—accomplished and well-educated, major or primary contributors to household finances—had experienced, or were still experiencing, abuse at the hands of their partners. Most were also raising children. All had suffered emotionally and often financially during their lengthy bad relationships. Some were determined to take their secrets to the grave. Others, like me, were ready with the right encouragement to break free.

Few of the women I spoke to remained cool or remote while I told my story. It was as if floodgates had opened. "Me too!" they would say, and jump into the conversation to share their own experiences or those of friends. We actually joked, as early as 2009, long before anyone had heard of a hashtag, that we should get T-shirts with the phrase "Me too!" on them. This sort of sharing tends to separate women from men. Given the opportunity, we like to talk, to confess, to bare our emotions, so we can compare, dissect, analyze, and empathize. Troubled men typically look for ways to distract themselves. They bottle up their emotions or drown them with addictive behaviors, preferring to talk about their successes, like closing a boardroom deal or conquering the ski slopes.

I met many high-achieving friends, neighbors, colleagues, and acquaintances in my workplace, at conferences, and at social events. I interviewed some more formally in the process of writing this book. Every time I talked to another woman, I received a further push to complete this book, despite my numerous professional commitments. The reaction was always one of sheer enthusiasm and encouragement. "What a subject!" "Someone has to finally talk about us."

The comments, suggestions, and stories kept coming, and each conversation gave me greater insight. With some close friends, I was already familiar with their intimate details. With others, a casual chat about my divorce over coffee led to a stream of revelations. Some neighbors and colleagues approached me directly, after my divorce, to ask for advice. Finally, some stories emerged from a forum I held at my home to which I invited a number of professional women to delve into this issue.

My patients, who come to me for pain management, often say they love the anecdotes I use to illustrate their issues. I'm a simple storyteller. Life is the master writer. Although I've changed names and some details for reasons of privacy, these are real-life accounts of women who have endured abusive relationships.

Sophia

I met Sophia at a professional conference in 1997, a couple of years after finalizing my turbulent divorce. As we chatted over coffee in a hotel bar, we noted the similarity of our upbringing. Sophia had been born and raised in Naples, Italy, by devout Catholic parents.

Her father, a successful Sicilian businessman, was a strict patriarch whose word was law. Her mother, who came from a wealthy
northern Italian family, was a well-educated housewife, involved
in philanthropy and music. Sophia deeply loved and respected her
father, at the same time as she resented his iron reign over the family and his unyielding Catholic morality. She also felt sorry for her
submissive mother, who had never been allowed to develop personal
or financial independence by working outside the home.

Sophia was considered a square peg in a round hole—the family's
black sheep because of her stubbornness, her sky's-the-limit goals,
and her dislike of strict religious beliefs and traditional family struc-
tures. While she had only a few school friends, her quiet, pleasant
brother, Antonio, was obedient and popular. Sophia excelled at her
studies but was considered disrespectful to her teachers because she
challenged their authority. In her last year of senior high school,
Sophia fell for a handsome classmate who was the sole heir to a family fortune. On the surface, the relationship looked good. In reality,
her fiancé was jealous, overbearing, demanding, rigid, and, worst of
all, deeply bothered by Sophia's intelligence and academic success.

When Sophia announced she was going to medical school, all
hell broke loose but she persevered. Her fiancé was mean and sometimes physically abusive. He isolated Sophia from her friends and
classmates. Weeks before her graduation, she discovered she was
pregnant, although she and her fiancé had used condoms. Sophia
freaked out. Her fiancé rejoiced. Now he held her captive. Catholics
do not have abortions.

Rebelling against both her fiancé and her strict religious upbringing, Sophia found a gynecologist willing to do an abortion and,
accompanied by a girlfriend, traveled to his shabby clinic in a different city. That butcher's work nearly caused her to bleed to death
and did enough damage to make her future pregnancies difficult.
She nevertheless graduated summa cum laudae. Sophia's fiancé

abandoned her because of the abortion. So did her family, when they found out.

Sophia moved to the United States, where she specialized in neurology, winning prestigious grants for her research work. On a cruise, she met a man her age, born in Toronto to a traditional Italian family. They married and settled in Toronto, where they had two daughters who, by the time I met their mother, were six and seven and a half. Sophia confessed to me that after ten years of marriage, she realized she had fallen into the same trap she had escaped in Italy. Her husband, his mother's favorite child, was domineering, rigid, spoiled, jealous, and insensitive. He envied Sophia's success and financial independence.

During a Sunday in early July, when Sophia's girls were at summer camp, Sophia told her husband that she had fallen out of love with him but wished to remain friends for the sake of the girls. She swore, truthfully, that no third party was involved and that the decision was hers alone. For days, he questioned her about the whys and hows, but Sophia was clear that his behavior had drained her of love and she was not prepared to spend the rest of her life with him.

That was the story Sophia confided in me as we chatted over coffee in our conference's hotel bar. Because she now looked up to me as the strong one, who was "already saved" while she was still overwhelmed by fear, doubt, despair, and confusion, we exchanged contact information, promising to keep in touch.

Back in Toronto, about a week after the conference, Sophia received several hang-up calls on her private office line. Feeling a sense of dread, she rushed home after her busy clinic hours. As she entered the kitchen, she saw blood splashed over the counter, the door, and the corridor walls, leading to the living room. There, she found her husband, face down on the floor with an empty vodka bottle by his side, streaks of blood staining the carpet. He had cut deeply into the veins of his forearms with a razor and was nearly unconscious or, more accurately, dead drunk.

Sophia's first action was to feel for a neck pulse. Her second was to call 911. Then she called me. I rushed to meet her at the local hospital emergency room. After Sophia's husband's wounds had been stitched up, he was committed to a psychiatric ward for just one day, then released to Sophia's care with this diagnosis: "Depression leading to a suicide attempt due to marital breakdown." Sophia was devastated. Though she felt terribly guilty, she was even more certain that her feelings for him were gone for good.

Sophia suggested her husband take a month-long trip to Italy, where he had relatives, to allow them time apart. With the help of her counselor, she broke the news of the impending divorce to her daughters, who had now returned from their month-long camp. She also prepared a full separation and divorce proposal to discuss with her husband upon his return. Since Sophia had been the family's sole financial supporter for the last five years, she offered her husband all the proceeds from the sale of the matrimonial home, their only asset, and 50/50 custody of their daughters. When Sophia's husband returned from his trip, his depression had transformed into sheer hatred, combined with a desire for revenge. He accused Sophia of having had many lovers and of stashing large amounts of money in foreign tax havens. Within two days, he maxed out their joint credit card, hired an expensive lawyer, and started a search for her imaginary secret lovers and hidden fortune.

Because the couple continued to cohabit during the acrimonious divorce, Sophia's house became the site of frequent police visits. Strangely, her husband was the one who usually called them. On one occasion, he told the police that Sophia planned to kill him. When they asked with what, he pointed to a small can of pepper spray that Sophia carried to protect herself as she crossed the dark hospital parking lot on nights when she worked late. One evening at dusk, Sophia came to my place, distraught. Her lawyer had informed her that her husband was demanding full custody of their daughters, along with the matrimonial home, where he was still living, and a sizable alimony. He claimed she was never at home, that he was the house-husband who took care of the kids, and that she was emotionally unstable, with a need for constant counseling.

"We've already had three mediations and two court hearings," Sophia exclaimed. "My life is shattered. He doesn't let me talk to the girls or pick them up from school. Every day, he spills garbage over the driveway or the kitchen floor so I have to clean it up. He has his buddies call my office, pretending they're from the RCMP, terrorizing my secretary and insisting I am under investigation for tax evasion."

She paused to brush away tears. "I feel so unsafe. He drinks heavily and has spells of incredible anger. He took photos of my underwear that he made into posters to share with his friends. The other day, I found him sharpening a huge knife. Shaking his head, he said, 'I should kill you, but I do not want to spoil my knife with a whore's blood.'"

I was freaking out as I listened to Sophia. "Let's go to the police. You can't live under siege. How are you functioning at work?"

"Barely," she answered, "but if I don't work, who will feed my children and pay the bills? What if I reveal this to the police, and they put him in jail? What would my girls think? What would the neighbors say?"

Sophia's cheeks were soaked in tears, her hands were shaking, her voice cracking. I shivered, recalling my own situation some years ago. How could all of this be happening to such an intelligent, accomplished woman? How had I allowed these things to happen to me, only two years ago? Sophia still had a long, brutal journey ahead, but today she is a free and independent woman, with full custody of her two children.

It was Sophia's story, so similar to my own, that made me realize that our experiences might be more common than either of us thought. How many others, women within my own circle of friends and acquaintances, were facing the same danger, the same shame, caught up in the same entrapment?

Nancy

For more than a decade, I had met with Nancy, a West Coast physiotherapist, at conferences across Canada and the United States. An elegant woman who took care of her health and appearance, Nancy was a multigenerational Canadian, born in Toronto. She and her three brothers were university educated and had successful careers. While at university, Nancy fell in love with and married a second-generation Portuguese dentist, who developed a large practice. By 2006, when Nancy approached me at a conference with a request to speak privately, they had a twelve-year-old son and a fourteen-year-old daughter.

As we settled into a private place in the lobby, Nancy said with excitement in her voice, "Listen, Angela, I know we don't speak often, but I must tell you, I have that article about you pinned up in my bedroom."

I was confused. "What article?"

"The one about you in the *National Review of Medicine* with a photo of you on your motorcycle."

For that publication's November 15, 2005, issue, I had been interviewed at home and in my office about my life as a busy professional, my black belt in Tae Kwon Do, and my newfound love for my Harley. It was rather a sensational piece, used as the center spread of a medical newspaper that is sent to thousands of doctors around the country. Apparently, Nancy had picked it up at her doctor's office while awaiting her annual checkup.

"My dream," Nancy continued, "has always been to ride my own motorcycle. I just did my safety course and now I have my license."

"That's cool!" I exclaimed. "What does your husband think?"

"He thinks I'm going through a midlife crisis, but then he never likes or approves of what I do." Nancy suddenly jerked forward on the sofa. Her face creased into a deep frown. "My only problem is my terrible back pain. I've suffered from it for years, so I can't imagine being able to ride a motorcycle."

A year later, at another conference, Nancy asked me to join her for dinner. Judging by her tone, it seemed she needed to talk. She did. Nancy spoke again of her still-unfulfilled dream of riding a motorcycle and then veered into talking about her unhappy marriage. She described her husband as jealous and controlling with explosive spells of anger and name-calling against both her and their kids. His anger was also causing trouble with his clinical staff, and even with the family's neighbors.

After one argument with Nancy about some insignificant matter, he had thrown a nightstand from a second-floor bedroom window. During another, he had struck Nancy.

"That's unacceptable!" I replied. "What are you doing about this?"

"I've been thinking about leaving him," replied Nancy, "but I'm worried about my job. I still have excruciating episodes of back pain, and lately, they've gotten worse. If I can't work, how can I support myself?"

Turning professional, I began to interview Nancy the way I would any patient. When did your back pain start? How often did it happen? Did it travel down your legs? What provoked it? What tests have you had? What kind of doctors or therapists have you seen?

"I've been diagnosed as having some wear and tear in my back," explained Nancy, "but the specialists don't understand why my pain is so bad."

Having encountered many cases like Nancy's, I asked, "Have you considered your pain might be the result of serious stress in your life? Do you suppose that might be what's tightening your muscles?"

Nancy paused. "I was afraid you'd say something like that. I've thought the same thing myself."

We spoke for hours, during which Nancy promised to seek counseling. After that, I did not see her for four years, leaving me to wonder what had happened to her. Then, at a 2011 Canadian Pain Society conference, Nancy sought me out once again. She was sporting tight leather pants and boots, worn with a noticeable air of confidence.

"Wow, you look good!" I said.

"I feel good," she replied.

With the help of a counselor, Nancy had found enough inner strength to face her problems and to ask her husband for a divorce. It had not been easy. He had furiously contested it, but a few months ago she had obtained her freedom and joint custody of the kids.

"By the way, I'm picking up my baby next week," she told me.

"Your baby?"

"My first Harley, a brand-new, sleek Dyna Low Rider." She added, with a sly smile: "My back pain is nearly gone."

Martha

Martha was a teacher at the Greek elementary school my two sons attended every Saturday. She was a short, slim, well-educated woman, who seemed very composed. When I picked up my kids, we often chatted. Since I had just rented a home, after obtaining full custody, I felt free to explore new friendships, so I invited Martha for dinner, along with her two sons, who were similar in age to my own. As the kids played in the basement, I mentioned how much I was enjoying my new freedom after my lengthy, dirty, and expensive divorce. Tears welled in Martha's eyes, as she opened her heart to describe her long years of verbal and emotional abuse. Her husband's infidelity, his broken work record, his lies, and his unreasonable spending habits all added to her mix of anguish.

"So, why are you still in this relationship?" I asked.

"My God," she replied, "what would my family think?"

Martha was caught in the trap of a conservative cultural tradition so common for people of Southern European origin. She believed she should keep her shame a secret, the same thought that had kept me quiet for years. She was also worried about being single again.

Years later, when I reconnected with Martha, I discovered that she was indeed divorced, not because she had walked out but because her husband had abandoned her to marry a much younger woman. Unfortunately, this had turned her into a sad, bitter woman whose experiences had aged her precipitously.

Anna Maria

Emotional abuse is not always perpetrated by a spouse. Other members of a close-knit family can victimize one half of a couple while the other spouse bears passive witness. Anna Maria was a Quebec product manager in the pharmaceutical industry, married to Gino and employed in the same industry. Since Anna Maria and I were both involved with projects relating to chronic pain, we became friends some years after my divorce.

Anna Maria considered her husband, who was Canadian-born with an Italian heritage like her own, to be a great partner and a caring father to their two kids, aged three and six. The problem was Anna Maria's in-laws. For years, she had suffered their incessant insults, impositions, and putdowns. On one occasion, they had entered Anna Maria's home while she and Gino were at work, and fired their nanny without permission or consultation. They often commented negatively and brutally on Anna Maria's appearance, cooking abilities, and child-rearing skills—and even on the way she had organized her kitchen.

I asked the question anyone would ask, "What does your husband do about all of this?"

"Nothing," Anna Maria replied. "He is devoted to his parents and never stands up for me."

Every time I spoke to Anna Maria over the next two years, she related another infuriating incident concerning her in-laws. Each time, I pointed out that this was emotional abuse and that her husband bore significant responsibility for allowing it to happen. I also advised her to seek counseling with her husband.

Though Anna Maria never did follow my advice, life may have given her a blessing in disguise. When her parent company underwent major restructuring, both she and Gino lost their Quebec jobs. After he was offered a good position in Vancouver, they moved to the West Coast, knowing Anna Maria stood a good chance of also finding employment in her field. I only hope the in-laws from hell did not move there as well.

A Gathering of Souls

My mission to collect more stories caused me to invite nine professional women to a forum at my house. All were friends, except for one, who came as a friend of a friend. I knew that some had been involved in bad relationships. Others had acquaintances who were in bad relationships. Only three in the group already knew each other. I had told each one about my book and that I wished their input for the project.

To make sure we were all on the same page, I had sent them a list of questions we would be discussing: What are the reasons we fall into unhealthy or destructive relationships? Why do we stay in unhealthy relationships? What coping strategies do we use to sustain us in a bad relationship? How do we get out of a bad relationship? What is our emotional aftermath—both positive and negative feelings—after escaping a bad relationship? What practical issues do we face as singles? If we want a new relationship, how do we find it? If you are already in a new relationship, how did you meet? Is it better than your last one and, if so, why? How should we interact with, and explain what is happening to, our kids throughout this process? We met one cold November evening in 2008 to offer opinions and to exchange experiences for my book. Though my guests were similar in age (from the mid-forties to the late fifties), we were an ethnically and professionally diverse group.

Rosa was Canadian-born with an Italian heritage. In her early fifties, she worked as a professional facilitator, providing enrichment experiences for professional organizations. Josie, from Guyana, was also in her early fifties. As a mediations specialist, she was in charge of employer/employee relations. Loretta, a multi-generational Canadian, was a corporate executive, in her late fifties. Gordana, born in Croatia, was a university-educated saleswoman in her mid-forties. Marina, born in Hong Kong, was a certified general accountant, in her early fifties. Eva, a multigenerational Canadian and a university administrator, was in her mid-fifties. Sophia, Italian-born, was a neurologist in her mid-fifties. Lori, a patient of mine in her forties, and Margarita, a clinic coordinator, my age, were both happily married, but they shared other people's stories with us.

Our conversation that evening was unguarded, inspirational, lively, and informative. Throughout the rest of this book, you will meet these women as they share their stories, opinions, and experiences.

CHAPTER 4

The Ties That Bind Us

ALL OVER THE WORLD, people hoping to fall in love experience mental fireworks, racing hearts, and sleepless nights. For many women, finding Mr. Right is a lifelong mission. Sometimes we measure our whole existence by the romanticized ideals of love portrayed in movies and romance novels. But with a bad relationship, the grim realities soon emerge, turning a fairy tale into a nightmare. The initial feelings of unbridled enthusiasm that hide the reality from us are not exclusive to the women I describe in this book. When we stick to a precarious relationship the problems mount. So why do we do it?

The main reasons for entrapment in an abusive relationship are as follows: low self-esteem, codependency, fear of being alone, lack of experience, shame (in its many faces), pressure from family or culture or religion, an excess of empathy, a misguided desire to please or nurture or rescue, concern for the welfare of the children, and money troubles. Let us discuss them one at a time.

Low Self-Esteem

I daresay this is the mother of all causes. I strongly believe low-esteem was pivotal in the destructive relationships of all the high-functioning women in this book, including my own. Most of us were happy with our work selves. In the boardroom, in laboratories, in law courts, we thrived. Many of us broke glass ceilings, earning the respect of our colleagues, both male and female. We worked effectively with other professionals, we were admired for our skills and leadership abilities, and sometimes we were also the primary or sole providers for our families. It was never the professional part of us that felt deficient. It was our feminine selves who felt small, weak, timid, insecure, and unwomanly, allowing our abusers to control us. Low self-esteem fueled other negative feelings, like fear of loneliness, a flawed perception of how we were viewed, and a fixation on belonging and being wanted.

I struggled for years to understand the origins of my own low self-esteem. Many of the other women with whom I spoke were clearly deprived of love during their childhood; they lived in abusive environments or perhaps were abused themselves. In my family, I was not unloved or neglected; I was treated like the jewel in the crown. My parents supported my intellectual accomplishments along with my talent for art and poetry. It was my sister who remembers feeling like a second-class citizen.

It was not until after my divorce that I explored the more subtle issues in my family that may have accounted for my insecurity. While I believe my father was devoted, he did not know how to show affection, either physically or verbally. My mother possessed numerous dependencies and unmet needs, which she did not hide. As a toddler, I was skinny, with huge hooded eyes, underlined with black circles. I compulsively sucked my right thumb until I was eleven, hiding in corners of the house just to stuff it into my mouth. During my preschool years, my mother covered my hands with gloves at night, but by morning I would have torn them off. She wrapped my thumbs in gauze soaked in quinine, a very bitter liquid. That did not work either. I would awaken with swollen lips and a black tongue. My explanation to our old neighborhood physician was, "some demon inside makes me do it."

Once, when I was nine, I dozed off on the subway with my head on my mother's shoulder, sucking my thumb. A strange voice awakened me. An old woman was chiding my mother. "Bad, bad habit!" She shook her head in disgust. "Nobody will marry her if she goes on like this." Embarrassed for both of us, my mother covered my face. Since I remember this incident almost half a century later, it must have made an impact on me, but I do not think it was the only one that caused me to curtail my "demonic" thumb-sucking at age eleven. Definitely, that habit was a sign of the tremendous anxiety and insecurity that riddled me.

If thumb-sucking had been the only demon in my life, I would have been a very lucky girl. I can remember, as young as age three or four, feeling intensely lonely and unwanted by the world (save for my immediate circle of parents, uncles, and aunts). I wonder, now, if this feeling might have been deeply rooted in my personality. Recent research has uncovered genes for aggression and monogamy in human beings. Could a gene for low self-esteem also exist?

I believe, now, that my early jealousy of my popular sister emanated from my deep feelings of inadequacy. It took me decades to understand that. Pari was a sweet, pleasant, considerate team player. I was dying inside to belong, but my personality was not getting me there. Mama would coax my sister's friends to include me in their play, but then she would have to rush out of the house to reprimand me, exasperated, for pushing another kid during hopscotch or ordering the others around during hide-and-seek. She would demand, "Who the hell would want to play with you, just to be bossed around?"

Poor Pari was frequently the victim of my bullying wrath. Many times, I slammed the door on her fingers or left bite marks on her arms. Her crime? Merely being liked by her peers while I was not. When I started writing this book I discussed with my sister my extremely aggressive early behavior. By then, I understood that immense insecurity was at the core of my jealousy. Attempting to exhaustively self-analyze can leave us more frustrated and confused than before. But what remains certain is this: my already low self-esteem plummeted during my first marriage, thanks to my husband's constant insults. He also attacked my emotional and spiritual identity, until I rescued myself and then built a new identity allowing no room for self-debasement.

Colette

Low self-esteem can be generalized or focused on a part of the self. For most of the women whose stories I looked at, it was our undeveloped feminine selves that made us feel insecure. However, even among high-achieving women, inferiority can center on the intellect if a woman feels her husband is much more clever than she is.

Colette was a beautiful, petite woman from Quebec, who held a responsible job at a big technology company. Nevertheless, she confessed to me during a business dinner, she felt intellectually inadequate when she compared herself to her husband, a high-ranking bank manager with a controlling grip on her. From their first meeting, her admiration for his intellect had made her overlook the huge differences of personality and temperament between them. Colette knew she was physically attractive, claiming center stage wherever she went, but it was not until much later that she realized she was smart enough not only to hold her own with her husband's friends but to achieve a position of power in her tech company. As she explained, "Once I found my brain, I lost much of my love for my husband. That shift allowed me to have an unfiltered view of the tremendous differences between us, most in my favor."

Although Colette's story differs from that of many other high-achieving women I talked to, she experienced the same marital inequality: her husband's intellectual control, and her dependency, until she rid herself of her delusion.

Codependency

Codependency is a type of learned behavior, also known as relationship addiction. People with codependency help to sustain relationships that are emotionally destructive or abusive. The term was originally used to describe a relationship with a chemically dependent partner (one addicted to drugs or alcohol). Today, the term has been broadened to include a relationship to a partner with other addictions (to sex, food, gambling, and so on), as well to a partner who suffers from a mental illness or a personality disorder, resulting in physical, emotional, or sexual abuse of the enabling person.[13]

Codependency is learned in childhood by observing adults in a dysfunctional family, where one member has an addiction or a mental disorder. Codependent members suffer from anger, fear, emotional pain, or shame that is unacknowledged, even denied. They learn to repress their emotions, focusing instead on taking care of the abusive person, placing that person's needs and well-being above their own.

Rosa

Rosa, who attended my forum, was born in Toronto to Italian parents who emigrated to Canada in the 1950s. She described her father as "a quiet alcoholic who drank himself to death," while her mother was tough, grouchy, and difficult. Rosa was surprised to learn, when discussing my forum questions with her mother, that she had sometimes been physically abused by Rosa's father.

In her early twenties, Rosa fell in love with Emilio, who came from a wealthy, traditional Italian family and who was "extremely spoiled with poor coping skills." Within the first five years of their marriage, they had a daughter and a son. Rosa completed two master's degrees and then developed a lucrative practice as a creative facilitator, providing enrichment experiences for large professional organizations.

Emilio, she discovered, had a cocaine addiction. When Emilio was high, he was hyperactive and unmanageable. Coming down, he was miserable. In between these states, Rosa described him as "perfect, loving, sensitive, and fun to be around." Due to Emilio's erratic behavior, the couple split and reconciled a few times. Each time Rosa sold their house, and each time she took Emilio back, she bought another one. Within six years, she had sold and bought three houses, incurring substantial financial losses each time. Their permanent split did not occur until Emilio tried to borrow money from their son's friends to support his habit.

After that, Rosa left for the final time, taking the kids. She sold that marital home as well. Though Rosa had ambivalent feelings about her split, she was managing reasonably well until she learned, six months after her separation, that Emilio was already with another woman. At that point, she collapsed, lost weight, and fell into such a profound depression that on many mornings she could not get out of bed. This competent professional, who made her living advising and guiding others, had to have intense psychotherapy. Teary-eyed, she explained to her counselor: "After so many years, I fixed him, and now another woman reaps the benefits!"

The therapist recommended that Rosa read *Co-dependent No More* by Melody Beattie. Rosa followed her counselor's advice, devoured every page several times over, and managed to put herself back together. By the time she came to our forum, she was involved in a fulfilling relationship. Unfortunately, her son usually took his father's side because he felt sorry for him as the underdog.

Carol

Several years ago, I befriended Carol, a woman in her early forties who was a high-ranking administrator at a major U.S. granting agency. Though I did not know it at the time, her multigenerational American family had been seriously dysfunctional, with noisy parental fights followed by emotional coldness. Carol had married an internationally known doctor; whenever I saw them at social functions, they seemed to have a calm, mutually fulfilling relationship.

One evening, while I was sharing a suite with Carol at a U.S. conference, she asked if she could have private use of the phone to call her husband, Gerald. As she explained, they had an agreement whereby whoever was away during their busy careers would call home every night. I closed the bedroom door and sat in the lounge of our suite. After a few minutes, I heard Carol's voice growing louder, although I could not hear her words. After about forty-five minutes, I heard Carol crying, causing me to realize that she and Gerald must have had an argument. When she came out of the bedroom, her eyes were red and swollen. When I asked if she was all right, she broke down.

Carol confessed that her famous husband suffered from bipolar disorder (a psychiatric condition in which a person fluctuates between very low and very high moods) and that he was also a fairly heavy drinker. The incident I had observed was part of a pattern of behaviors that varied according to Gerald's moods. The two of them would start out by talking about some simple matter—for example, what Carol had learned at the conference—and then one of them would say something that would be misinterpreted by the other. The conversation would spiral out of control into "I said, you said" accusations, followed by anger and sadness.

Carol confessed that her tears at the end of a call often resulted from Gerald's ramming the phone into its cradle, or throwing it to the ground and kicking it. Still, not phoning him was inconceivable to her. The next evening, Carol mumbled to me how much she hated calling Gerald, then insisted she had to do it. Once again, she participated in a lengthy, unhappy conversation.

These phone calls were only part of Carol's troubled relationship. She confided that she and Gerald had a joint account that neither could use without the other's approval. This led to fights and days in which words were barely exchanged, unless they had to show up for some event, where they appeared as the perfect couple.

Carol had thought of divorce many times, but said she was afraid of hurting her husband. Years later, I discovered that the couple had split after nineteen tumultuous years of marriage. Carol told me that when she finally found the courage to suggest divorce to Gerald, he was relieved. He had been feeling just as discontent with their marriage.

Codependency lies at the core of many dysfunctional relationships. No doubt, it factored into mine.

Fear of Being Alone

Another issue contributing to our self-imposed captivity is the daunting thought of being single again, with its accompanying fear of loneliness. As I have already explained, that demon had a strong grip on me, beginning when I was a toddler. During the forum at my home, all ten of us agreed that if we loved ourselves and believed in our own worth we would never feel alone. But loving one's self after being in an abusive relationship is a long, hard process.

It took me years to learn to self-love. Achieving it does not mean giving up the desire or need for others. Today, I spend a great deal of time with my kids, my friends, and my second husband, not out of neediness but because I value their company. At the same time, being on my own provides a welcome opportunity to relax and to breathe.

Nureem

Nureem, a twenty-six-year-old physician, befriended me in 1980, during my physical medicine residency at a teaching hospital where she was chief medical resident. Born in India, Nureem had traveled the globe with her father, a foreign diplomat from an Asian country, and her British mother. She spent her high school and early university years in England and then settled in Canada to pursue her medical career.

Everything about Nureem exuded a mystical, exotic air. She was 5′2″ tall and slim, with olive skin, straight black hair to her waist, and emerald eyes that dominated her face. She reminded me of a wildcat as she both moved and spoke quickly in her elegant, British accent. She was also a smart, outspoken go-getter.

When Nureem visited me in my little bachelor apartment, we talked about our personal lives. My husband Johnny was still in Greece and Michael, who was Nureem's boyfriend of two years, was a senior orthopedic resident at another teaching hospital. He was Canadian-born, athletic, and very good-looking, the sort of high-status partner for whom most women yearn. Nureem spoke of him fondly and seemed happy with their relationship.

One day, Nureem came to my place with her left arm in a cast, claiming she had slipped in the snow. A few months later, she was on crutches, with her broken leg in a cast, another unfortunate slip in the snow. It was not until several months into our friendship that

Nureem invited me to her home. As we sat on her porch, surrounded by azaleas, she asked me to listen to a message on her answering-machine. I heard Michael leave a loving, longing message asking her to call him back. In a second message that followed immediately, Michael demanded in an angry, aggressive voice why Nureem had not returned his call. He then began to threaten her. More messages followed, minutes apart, laden with name-calling, during which Michael grew ever more hostile. He accused Nureem of having another lover and threatened to break her legs as well as to harm her in other ways. I was dumbfounded.

In Nureem's words, her relationship with Michael had "gotten out of hand." He was extremely jealous, dominating, and abusive, both verbally and physically. She had, twice before, ended up with fractured limbs from Michael's atrocious acts of violence. His violence had also included slapping, hair-pulling, face-punching, throwing her to the ground, and choking her in a jealous rage. Nureem confided that she had recently obtained a court order to keep Michael away. However, as my lawyer would tell me years later during my own divorce, "Court orders are only respected by law-abiding citizens, not crazy ones."

Sure enough, Michael continued to stalk Nureem, violating not one but two court orders. As well as leaving the threatening answering-machine messages, he had staked out her house. Even I felt scared, thinking he might suddenly appear as we sat on Nureem's porch.

I asked Nureem if she had talked to the authorities where Michael was chief resident or reported him to the College of Physicians and Surgeons of Ontario, our regulatory body for administering doctors' licenses.

"Certainly not!" she responded. "I don't want to destroy his career."

During the following years, I lost track of Nureem. However, a mutual acquaintance told me she had reconciled with Michael, and that the two had left the province after finishing their specialty training. I often wondered if Nureem was still with Michael or if she had left him. More importantly, I asked myself if Nureem was still alive.

Five years ago, thirty-five years after Nureem had disappeared from my life, I learned of her whereabouts through a twist of fate. A patient of mine, with nerve damage from a broken leg, informed me that Nureem was a friend of hers. Nureem had, indeed, married Michael, and they had had a son. Five years later, Michael had left Nureem for another woman whom he eventually married. Nureem was now practicing medicine in another province, mourning "the loss of the love of her life."

According to this patient, she was a broken woman. The patient gave me Nureem's contact information, but, sadly, Nureem never returned my voice messages or emails and I stopped trying to reach her. Obviously, she had no desire to talk to me, likely feeling burdened by shame. For Nureem, emotional and physical abuse was the price she was willing to pay for Michael's companionship, but she was nonetheless abandoned. Nureem's story left a frightening mark on my memory.

Sandy

I met Sandy, a multigenerational Canadian nurse in her early forties, when she was head of the obstetrical unit of a downtown hospital where we were both taking a professional course. When she came to my office to pick up some course materials, she saw the photographs of my boys behind my desk. As one question led to another, I took this opportunity to tell her of my recent divorce and to extol my newfound freedom. By now, I knew that the ease with which I discussed my failed marriage opened the door for others to confess to marital problems.

Sandy had just initiated divorce proceedings against her husband, a freelance photographer with a scant work record and a taste for expensive clothes and cars. During the past two years of their ten-year marriage, his constant barrage of insults about her appearance and everything she said or did had become unbearable. "Thank God we don't have any kids!" she said, close to tears. "I wonder who else will ever want to be with me?"

Sandy was not at her best: her appearance screamed neglect. Her insecurity was understandable.

"Listen, you do have to take better care of yourself," I replied in my usual to-the-point manner. I then gave Sandy the same advice I had given myself. "Don't even think about a new relationship until you have received some emotional help, some fitness training, and perhaps some professional advice about clothes and makeup. If you learn to like yourself, others will follow suit."

I handed Sandy *The Verbally Abusive Relationship* by Patricia Evans. She thanked me, promising to report back. Three months later, Sandy handed my secretary the Evans book, along with a quick note: "Thank you, very helpful."

When I flipped through the pages, I noticed six of the seven-item list determining one's level of abuse had been checked in blue ink. I had checked only five, in black. When I tried to call Sandy, I found her number had been changed. She never contacted me again. Much later, I found she had resigned her current hospital job for one in another city.

Lack of Experience

I cannot count the number of times high-achieving women have blamed their willingness to stay in a bad relationship on their youthful naivety: "I didn't know what I was doing, I had no experience."

Far too often, entering too young into a long-term relationship is a setup for failure. We go to school to learn to read and write, but who teaches us what to look for in a partner? Much of the time, our parents did not know, themselves, so what they mirrored for us was likely their own mistakes. Most of the women in my forum agreed on this point. The youthful experience of falling in and out of love, of hurting and being hurt, of being wanted and then rejected made women tougher and more resilient when it came to making lifetime choices. Without such experiences, we remain too soft and vulnerable. Like the measles virus, catch it early and you develop immunity. Miss that immunity and it can become a serious disease. Out of the eight couples who married from my high-school class, six, including me, were divorced by the late 1990s.

Michelle

Canadian-born Michelle, of British heritage, was a vibrant, attractive, outspoken, highly respected physician in her mid-fifties with whom I served on scientific committees. She was also a sports coach for young people, including her two teenaged daughters. She often said that if she were not a doctor, she would have chosen a career in coaching.

Since I knew Michelle was divorced, I talked to her about my own experiences and found her absolutely forthcoming. Michelle's ex-husband, Joshua, had enjoyed a life of leisure, since, as she put it, he had "the goose who laid the golden eggs at home." When I asked Michelle why she thought women like us fall into these marital messes and stay there, she replied, "Because we were so busy focusing on our careers that we never acquired experience of the dating field. We had 'sucker' written on our foreheads, so predators could easily find us."

Michelle had four sisters. "My mother, who was a successful professional, pushed all five of us to obtain university degrees. We were not exposed to dating like other girls. We were consumed by our studies. The net result? Out of the five of us—all successful career women—three of us were in long-term abusive relationships before we managed to get out."

The Many Faces of Shame

Shame comes in many shades and variations for those of us in bad relationships: shame for having a miserable personal life; shame for having a private self so different from the one we show to our colleagues; shame for being the only provider in our household while pretending we are not; shame for having to admit to our parents and friends that they were right to oppose our marriage; shame for our weak heart in wanting to stay in our marriage when our head knows we must leave.

Once we victims break free, the first shame we relinquish is that of silence. Women like me usually feel at ease sharing, acknowledging, and dissecting our past, while those still stuck in abuse may quickly change the subject and refuse offers of help.

Kate

A trainee of mine, and a multigenerational Canadian in her late thirties, Kate disappeared rather suddenly from a project we were planning together. After I had not heard back from her, I became worried about her health, so I sent her a couple of emails. Weeks later, she briefly reported that she was in the process of dealing with a very bad marriage. This was no surprise to me. At social events, her husband would comment callously on how she was dressed and leave her alone while he drank with his buddies.

When I asked Kate if I could do anything for her, she emailed a dry response: "No, thanks. I told you what was going on just because I was advised to inform you why I am not pursuing the project anymore." When I suggested counseling, Kate replied, "Not for now. My kids and I are studying a number of books to figure out what went wrong. We don't need a counselor."

For Kate, the privacy of books was preferable to the shame of admitting, even to a therapist, that she had marital problems she could not solve.

Pressure from Family, Culture, or Religion

Across the globe, women's rights are routinely violated. Some are forbidden to drive cars, others are subjected to the barbaric practice of female circumcision, which involves amputation of the clitoris to assure faithfulness by preventing a woman's sexual pleasure. Because cultural or religious underpinnings govern these observances, different societies understand and define female abuse very differently. Psychologist Joan Lachkar reports that while American women perceive Muslim women in Saudi Arabia as abused because they submit to men and are considered chattels, Saudi women perceive their American counterparts as abused because they are forced to work while bringing up children, without the help of an extended family, in a society rife with drugs, violence, and divorce.[14]

Social, cultural, religious, and familial pressures play a powerful role in keeping many women in bad relationships. Concern about what others think is woven, to some degree, into all of our decisions, big or small. "Others" include not only our immediate family and friends, but also people in our workplaces and communities.

Though I now know of many Greek people my age and younger who have divorced, I was the first in my traditional, extended family to take this forbidden step. Even while I was going through the process, a male Greek-Canadian friend and neighbor insisted, "Drop all these crazy ideas and go back to your husband. Good Greek women do not leave their spouses!" Looking him straight in the eye, I told him, "This is my personal business. You have no idea what goes on in this household, and absolutely no right to give me instructions."

One professional woman told me that when she initiated divorce proceedings against her abusive husband, her family took his side. Since he had always been careful to victimize her in private, they did not believe her stories. After her divorce, her relatives disowned her for many years before finally understanding her situation. In the Western world, marriages between people of different races, religions, and cultures are increasingly common, resulting in clashes and conflicts not only between individuals but also between families and communities.

Poonam

One of my trainees, Poonam, was born in Toronto to Pakistani parents who had immigrated to Canada many years earlier. Her mother was a physician and her father an engineer. Poonam followed strict Muslim tradition and entered an arranged marriage with a compatriot of similar social class and education. Her husband proved to be autocratic, domineering, and jealous as well as verbally, sexually, and physically abusive. Poonam was torn between her Pakistani culture and Canada's more liberal attitudes. She wanted her husband to take counseling with her but he adamantly refused: "Real men do not see shrinks."

Despite the fact that Poonam possessed a degree in business administration and a well-paying managerial job at a large company, she was terrified at the thought of divorce and the reactions of her parents and family. Even now, after years of counseling, she continues to cycle through depression, yo-yoing weight gain and loss, as she attempts to strategize an exit from her marriage only to fall back into the same pattern.

Miranda

I routinely met Miranda, who is a lawyer, at dinner meetings of the Medico-Legal Society of Toronto, an association for the discussion of matters bridging medicine and law. The product of a well-heeled, multigenerational Canadian family, Miranda was a calm, soft-spoken, classy woman in her late forties, always dressed impeccably as if for the boardroom. Stylistically, I was Miranda's opposite; I like vibrant, expressive clothing. Despite our cultural and aesthetic differences, we clicked during these professional gatherings, which took place three or four times a year.

During one dinner meeting, I opened up about my past, sharing my journey of discovery. Miranda then felt comfortable about telling me her story, too. She had recently divorced an internationally known doctor, also from a well-established Canadian family, whom I knew by reputation. Though their marriage had been dysfunctional for a long time, Miranda had been too ashamed to admit to its failure; divorce was considered inappropriate for her class for reasons of social status, business relationships, and wealth. The adults belonged to the same clubs and served on the same arts and charity boards. Their kids went to the same private schools and summer camps.

After Miranda joined a big downtown law firm, her husband had become morbidly jealous of her success and the fact that she was making more money in personal-injury law than he did as a prestigious medical researcher. As Miranda described the conflicts between them, I realized her husband's polished, WASP background did not affect how he victimized her, only the sophistication of his mind games and his vocabulary. Once Miranda realized she was being emotionally abused, she could no longer tolerate the put-downs, the jealousy, or the emotional turmoil, despite pressure within her social circle to maintain her marriage for the sake of class solidarity.

After Miranda walked out, her story did not finish peacefully. Her husband sent vicious letters to her legal firm, trying to tarnish her reputation. He balked at the division of assets. He badmouthed her to mutual friends. He called her office to belittle her with child-ish name-calling and so forth. When Miranda purged her soul to me, she was still reeling from the aftermath of her hostile divorce. To encourage her, I told her about my own ongoing recovery. My kids were now in my full custody. I had paid outstanding taxes that had piled up during my court battles and had bought and renovated a small house. I was Latin-dancing twice a week and I was even involved in a new romantic relationship. Above all, I was at peace with myself because I liked the woman I had become.

Miranda looked at me with envy and said, "You know, I used to jog every day at the crack of dawn, but I haven't done it for a good three years. In university, I was a competitive long-distance runner."

"So, why don't you start again?" I encouraged her. "Your kids are about to finish high school. You don't have to be there at 6 a.m. to prepare breakfast anymore."

She looked at me with excitement in her eyes. "Maybe I should try it again."

Six months later, I saw Miranda at another meeting. As she came to my table, I noticed a glow about her and a sparkle in her eyes that had been missing during the three years I had known her. Her style was also more feminine; she was wearing a blue silk dress that complemented her hair and complexion.

"I did it!" she announced. "Angela, you are my role model. I started jogging again four months ago. Now I can't go a day without it, no matter how bad the weather. I haven't felt this good in such a long time."

Miranda's smile reflected her inner contentment. Years later, I learned that Miranda had become a senior partner in her legal firm. She was, by then, in a long-term relationship with a colleague and celebrating the fact that her daughter had made her a grandmother—a very good-looking grandmother, I must add.

Tassia

I want to make one last point about "cultural norms," meaning traditions, laws, and ideologies that may justify societal aggression, keeping women in abusive relationships.[15] My cousin Tassia is a lovely woman, who lives with her husband in a large city in southern Greece. Since they were financially comfortable, and both her kids had families and businesses, she took early retirement from teaching to look after her two grandchildren.

On my last trip to my homeland, I met up with Tassia and her husband while visiting my sister. As the men chatted, we three women went into the kitchen to prepare coffee and dessert. All of a sudden, Tassia's husband started yelling. "Where's this freakin' coffee? Can't you move your lazy ass?"

My cousin apologized to him, then hurried up our preparation. A few minutes later, he yelled again. This time, it was because he did not approve of how she had pacified her crying grandchild. I pulled my sister aside. "What the hell is going on with him? In my books, his behavior is abusive and intolerable."

My sister tried to placate me. "Don't mind him, he's just a screamer. He's actually a devoted husband, and when Tassia was sick, he took exceptional care of her."

Between my uncles and neighbors, I had known a lot of "screamers" while growing up in Greece. Their behavior had not bothered me until I embraced Canada's liberal values. Women from a variety of cultural backgrounds may find it difficult to know what is appropriate and what is not because of their cultural norms. In my experience, Mediterranean, Central European, and South American ethnic groups have traditions similar to my Greek ones. I cannot imagine how it must be in cultures known to be openly oppressive and degrading to women. When people from these cultures emigrate to Canada and other Western nations, there is a real potential for a clash of values within marriages, supported by sometimes isolated communities.

An Excess of Empathy

Research indicates that it is plausible that something inherent in our female nature contributes to women's acceptance of unhealthy relationships. In a study of couples conducted at the Institute of Neurology at University College London,[16] researchers administered electric shocks to the hands of women, while using an fMRI (functional magnetic resonance imaging machine) to read their brain activity. After noting the specific brain areas where the women experienced the painful shocks, they administered shocks to their male partners. When the women observed their partners receiving strong and weak shocks, their brain activity was exactly the same as when they were receiving the shocks themselves. When the researchers reversed the procedure, the men's brains did not respond to the shocks suffered by the women. In other words, the women were feeling their partners' pain, while the males did not reciprocate. This is one example of dramatic differences in the makeup of human sexes.

Empathy, feeling another person's pain as if it were your own, is different from sympathy, which means feeling for another person. Empathy is currently a major topic of human study. Back in the 1990s the discovery of mirror neurons in monkeys—brain cells that fire up both when a person performs an act and when they observe the same action performed by someone else—was heralded by some as one of the greatest neurological findings of the decade.[17] Mirror neurons have been found in the premotor cortex and the inferior parietal cortex, and they may exist in other brain areas as well. This constellation of mirror neurons is considered by some scientists to underlie human empathy, though the topic has raised both hype and controversy. Many factors can affect the strength of an empathetic brain response to pain, such as the degree of pain inflicted, the conditions under which the pain is inflicted, the identity of the person experiencing the pain, and the characteristics (male or female) of the person observing the process.

In another study, women were found to empathize with people who were punished for cheating in a game whether the punishment was unfair (because they had not cheated) or fair (because they had cheated). This all-encompassing empathy was not exhibited by men. In fact, their brains actually registered joy when fair punishment was meted out.[18] Several other studies, conducted by Chinese scientists using different neurophysiological measures, also confirmed the differences between men and women in regard to empathetic responses.[19] In a large cross-cultural study, researchers tested 485 children between the ages of seven and eleven from the United States, Northern Ireland, the Republic of Ireland, Germany, South Africa, and Israel (including Jewish and Arab children).[20] The subjects rated descriptive statements such as "not like me," "sort of like me," or "really like me." In a striking cross-cultural similarity, girls showed much higher levels of empathy than boys with differences emerging at around age ten in all participants except those from South Africa.

Empathy is not limited to humans. My colleague, Jeff Mogil from McGill University, conducted the first-ever study revealing seeds of empathy in mice, hundreds of times smaller and dramatically different neurologically from humans.[21] Mogil and his team injected acetic acid into the abdomen of mice, causing them pain, which they manifested as "writhing behavior." When two injected mice were able to see each other, they mutually displayed much higher levels of writhing behavior if they had previously been cage mates (meaning they had grown up in the same colony) than if they were strangers. This cage-mate behavior is an example of "emotional contagion." In higher primates, such as chimpanzees and humans, emotional contagion progresses to become empathy. It remains to be seen whether mice exhibiting this behavior experience the same kind of brain activity as humans do. If this is the case, perhaps empathy is the product of evolution in mammalian species.

In summary, scientific evidence suggests that empathy has a biological basis and that women are more sensitive to the feelings of others than are men. This natural capacity means that women in a bad relationship might willingly give much more than they receive.

Women as Pleasers, Nurturers, or Rescuers

Whether it is biological, psychological, sociological or all, women have a tendency to want to nurture and to please others. Too many of us thrive on the act of giving, while asking too little in return. This constant, unconditional giving was my problem until I sought professional help following my divorce. It pervaded all my close relationships, not just my marriage. Even today, my trainees call me a "mother hen." However, my motive in giving to them is simply because I feel I have the skill and the capacity to do so and because professional mentorship was never offered to me. Too much giving spoils the receiver, and undermines the giver by projecting the feeling that we believe we are unworthy of receiving.

Actress Jane Fonda called the empathy of her early years "the disease to please," as Susan Pinker reports in her 2008 book *The Sexual Paradox*. With me, even years after my divorce, accepting a gift brought tears to my eyes. Eventually I learned that, indeed, I did deserve to have others please me and even to please myself by treating myself. Sometimes this need to give translates into a desire to rescue our partners and to believe they could not survive without us. During my rocky marriage, one morbid idea always stopped me in my tracks whenever I thought of leaving: What will he do without me? His feelings and needs always took priority over mine.

Excessive nurturing is sometimes learned from our upbringing. My mother's early years spent looking after her own disabled mother was a pattern passed down to me, even though she felt resentful about her stolen youth. Like her, I mothered my partner, making a bad relationship worse.

Concern for the Welfare of the Children

Concern for our children is a fundamental bind that keeps many women in a destructive relationship, because we are much more likely than men are to place the children's welfare before our own. Female attachment to an infant is an innate property of motherhood, whereas male attachment is more a function of social learning.[22]

Again, this theory has been tested in the laboratory. If a male rat is given female hormones before his brain becomes fully "male," he will typically exhibit female parental behaviors. If a female rat is treated with male hormones early in her development, she will demonstrate very little maternal behavior.[23] Studies have shown similar results with human females who were exposed in the womb to high levels of male hormones, as in cases of polycystic ovarian syndrome. Such little girls refuse to play with dolls; as teens they don't babysit, and as adults they are uninterested in children.

This is not to say that men do not care about their kids. For some, parental bonding happens very early and instinctively, but for many it happens a bit later, when the kids are old enough to "do things" with their father like playing ball. When a crisis arises and a marriage breaks down, many more women than men will take full responsibility for their children—emotionally, physically, and financially. Children certainly fare better in two-parent households, provided the parents' relationship is balanced, constructive, and based on mutual respect, although, in the long run, the daily friction and arguments of a troubled relationship are more detrimental than being raised by a single, loving parent in a stable household.

My own case was complex, because I thought my ex-husband was a good father to our sons. He just happened not to be a good husband to me. It was only much later that I realized that abusing the mother of your children is antithetical to being a good parent. During our contentious divorce, Johnny used our boys as pawns, leaving emotional scars on their hearts that took years to heal. Thankfully, they matured into emotionally healthy young men, able to use their experiences constructively in forming their own partnerships.

At the forum at which I met with nine other women, we found that seven of us (victims of dysfunctional relationships) had paid the bills and were our kids' primary caretakers. However, of our combined total of thirteen kids, all young adults, five had sided with their fathers. In their eyes, their fathers were underdogs while their high-achieving mothers were to blame for walking out on them. Often this is a case of "absence makes the heart grow fonder." When mothers are constantly available and forgiving, they become "safe" targets for venting resentment, anger, fear, and grief over the divorce. Meanwhile, less available fathers become elusive, distant "others" with the option of ignoring their children or showering them with gifts. Their approval cannot be taken for granted. It must be gained by pleasing behavior. Hopefully, with greater maturity, the children of my forum friends will gain a fairer perspective.

Josie

Despite the pressures of family, religion, and culture, Josie finally felt she had no choice but to leave her family, including her children. Saving herself, she decided, was the best way to help them, much like donning one's own oxygen mask during a bumpy plane flight in order to best protect dependents. Josie, who attended my forum, was born in Guyana to a Christian family of East Indian descent. Several half-brothers, products of her father's infidelity with several women, joined Josie and her sister when Josie was nine. Josie's father was abusive to her mother, a wonderful, witty woman who encouraged Josie's educational ambitions.

When Josie was twelve, her father died. One of her half-brothers subsequently convinced Josie's mother to sign over control of their father's lucrative business. Due to his conniving, Josie, her mother, and her sister slipped from princesses to paupers in a short time. Fortunately, Josie's mother had her own small cleaning business, allowing Josie, at eighteen, to attend university in Toronto. There, Josie fell in love with Zora, a blue-collar Eastern European. After graduating from college, she married him, although his parents made it clear they disliked and disapproved of Josie as a woman of color.

After only a few months, Zora began a litany of demeaning comments. When their son was only sixteen months old, Josie arrived home earlier than expected to find Zora in bed with a coworker. During a stormy breakup, Zora kicked Josie and the baby out of the house, even though Josie, a mediations specialist in charge of employer/employee relations, was the primary breadwinner.

Josie's mother, who had joined her in Canada, attempted to patch up the relationship because she could not bear the idea of divorce. During a reconciliation, Josie became pregnant with her second son. Zora grew increasingly abusive, both verbally and physically. Though Josie was very attractive, he called her "fat and ugly." In one violent incident, he threw her down the stairs. When she called the police, she received no sympathy. "You didn't get hurt," they said, dismissing the incident as no big deal. Josie endured the abusive relationship mostly because of the pressure of her Christian friends, who felt it was her duty to tough out her marriage.

Even while building up her professional reputation, Josie grew terribly depressed and physically unwell. Eventually, the aching, burning pains throughout her body were diagnosed as fibromyalgia, a syndrome characterized by changes within the nervous system caused by physical or emotional stress. Zora's emotional pounding was relentless. After twenty years, Josie crashed. She wrote a farewell letter to her children and disappeared with only the clothes on her back. Two lawyers, three courts, and five years later, she obtained a costly divorce, leaving behind an almost fully paid house and agreeing to provide alimony and tuition for her children's education.

Tragically, Josie became involved in another abusive relationship, isolating herself from friends and dropping out of sight. Later, I heard from others that she did eventually free herself from that relationship too.

Money Troubles

Financial dependence is another big reason for staying in a destructive, long-term relationship. For high-achieving women, the problem is usually not their financial dependence but the dependence of their partners and their family on them. Based on Canadian family law, when a couple splits, both partners have to part with half the equity they acquired during the marriage. Additionally, after a few years, the matrimonial home is split in half, even if one spouse owned it in totality before the marriage. Exceptions are made only if the couple signed a prenuptial agreement. None of the women in this book did, so most of us had to pay our exes significant amounts to secure our divorces.

Sophia, my neurologist friend, is a prime example. Her ex insisted to the bitter end that he had been a full-time, stay-at-home parent. He dragged her from court to court asking for full custody of their two daughters—which, of course, went hand-in-hand with alimony, common expenses, and child support. After lengthy legal battles that consumed an inordinate amount of the couple's assets, the courts awarded Sophia and her ex fifty-fifty custody. He angrily rejected that decision because it left him with only half the money he had targeted. Within days of the court ruling, he walked away, giving Sophia full custody and taking limited alimony for a short, predetermined time. Sophia was also left with hefty bills from the expensive legal firm she had hired, along with two years of unpaid taxes. She owned no property and had no assets besides a leased car. Apart from the costs of legal proceedings, high-achieving women usually find that extreme stress cuts down on their ability to work at a time when they need more money to survive. Few of us have anything left to build a new life upon.

Stephanie

With my friend Stephanie, the comfortable lifestyle that her husband could provide and his reluctance to split his assets was one of the reasons that kept them both in a dysfunctional relationship. Born in Portugal and raised in Canada from age six, Stephanie married a well-known architect of similar ethnic origin. She used her business administration degree to work for him, part-time, handling his administrative matters while singlehandedly raising two daughters and a son.

After fifteen years of marriage, Stephanie suspected her husband was having an affair. A private investigator confirmed that he was supporting a lover in a fully paid apartment with other perks. Stephanie's family and her husband's family got together, like a family court, to confront the adulterous man. He admitted to his affair and promised to terminate it, but then did not keep his word.

If you've seen the comedic films *My Big Fat Greek Wedding* and *Mambo Italiano*, you'll have an idea of the closely woven structure of Stephanie's extremely traditional Catholic family. She was raised to see marriage as a stronghold, never to be broken. She was terrified of the shame of divorce and of its effect on her three children. In addition, she did not want to lose the lucrative lifestyle her husband's success afforded her. Stephanie's husband was also afraid that scandal would tarnish his reputation, resulting in a loss of clientele. He was even more firmly opposed to giving his wife half of his fortune, as required by Canadian family law, and then paying alimony and child support. Instead, the couple chose to remain married. They moved into separate bedrooms in their mansion while attending public functions together, still pretending to be happily married. At home, they hardly spoke except for loud exchanges of insults.

Stephanie's husband continued to pay the family bills, including those for lengthy holidays abroad for Stephanie and the children. She was free to stay out late on weekends, no questions asked.

Despite her "freedom," Stephanie fell into a horrible depression. She consulted a psychiatrist, who loaded her up with antidepressants. They did not seem to make much difference. She also came to me as a patient, complaining of severe generalized pain throughout her body. A rheumatologist had diagnosed her with fibromyalgia, a syndrome of excessive sensitivity and widespread pain. Since I had seen Stephanie's condition many times before, I suspected that a serious emotional stressor was likely at the root of her trouble.

"Your depression and your pain will never go away unless you change the circumstances of your personal life," I told Stephanie. Years later, I heard that she had fallen in love with a man whom she had met while on vacation in Portugal. After extending this holiday by many months, she came to see me. With her voice trembling in excitement, she told me she was crazy in love. Since these feelings were mutual, she and her lover constantly emailed and talked on the phone. When Stephanie announced the news to her husband, he had not taken it well, despite his own infidelities. Still, neither wanted to dissolve the marriage. "By the way, doc," Stephanie told me, "all my pain is gone, and I have dramatically cut down on my medications!"

Fear for Our Physical Well-being

Several of the women I spoke with lived in constant fear of being physically hurt. This primary issue binds many women to their unhealthy relationships. A woman is twice as likely to be violently victimized by someone with whom she is intimate than by a stranger. Women who leave abusive partners are seventy times more likely to be killed in the few weeks after leaving than at any other time in the relationship.[24]

The shocking story of Dr. Elana Fric-Shamji, who was murdered when she tried to leave her husband, puts a tragic face on that statistic. Often, battered women do not have anywhere to go. The United States has nearly three times as many animal shelters as it has shelters for battered women and their children.[25] Fifty per cent of all American homeless women and children take to living on the streets because of violence at home.[26]

The 1999 General Social Survey on victimization (GSS)[27] asked some 26,000 people in Canada if they had experienced some form of violence, from threats to assault, by a current or previous partner over a five-year period. Eight percent of women and 7 percent of men declared that they had, with the violence experienced by women being more severe and more frequent. Canadian women were also more likely than their partners to have experienced emotional abuse, such as being denied access to family income, having their possessions damaged, being isolated from family and friends, and being subjected to name-calling and putdowns.[28]

Factors that increased risk for abuse included being young (eighteen to twenty-four), being elderly (sixty-five or older), being disabled, being Indigenous, being pregnant, having been victimized in childhood, or having witnessed violence against one's mother.[29] During my friend Sophia's ten-year emotionally abusive relationship, she had never feared being physically hurt by her husband until she walked out of the marriage; that's when all hell broke loose. Because she was unwilling to live apart from her kids and unable to shoulder the additional expense of renting another place, she had to cohabit for two years with her husband until the divorce was final. Though she moved into a different bedroom, on many nights she lay trembling because her husband had threatened her with violence and would not allow her to put a lock on her door. She called the police several times. Even after Sophia's divorce was finalized, it took several years for her to stop shaking at the mere thought that her ex might be nearby or that he might be spying on her.

Georgia

I met Georgia, who is a few years younger than me, when I visited her downtown clothing store after deciding I wanted to learn how to dress well. Having grown up as a tomboy, I did not know how to apply makeup or coordinate colors. Georgia, who left Croatia thirty-five years ago, was a classically beautiful woman, slim and tall with long black hair and well-shaped eyebrows. Everything about her exuded elegance and good taste, including the clothes in her designer shop that caters to professional women. During the evolution of our friendship, I spoke to Georgia about the hardships of my divorce, which caused her to open up about her own story.

Georgia's Croatian husband, Goran, owned a small, struggling business that Georgia often had to support. He suffered low self-esteem, making him withdrawn and subject to spells of severe anger and intense jealousy. He often manifested this behavior in public, even while hosting Georgia's mother or other relatives. He routinely degraded Georgia with name-calling or by giving her the silent treatment. On a number of occasions, his anger became physical, causing him to toss around objects as well as to attack Georgia. He constantly threatened her life if she ever attempted to leave him and, because of their disconnect, they had not slept together in fifteen years.

These details startled me. "Why do you stay in this marriage? Why are you letting your youth slip away?"

"Fear," she replied, voice trembling. "I know what you went through during your divorce. My afflictions are already as severe without my attempting to escape."

Georgia was also concerned about the effects of a divorce on her son, adopted from Croatia when he was an infant. Since Georgia considered Goran a good father, she did not want to deny the boy a relationship with his dad. Like so many of the women I spoke with, Georgia could not see that making him a witness to an abusive relationship was the antithesis of being a "good" father. Finally, Georgia knew that a divorce would result in major financial losses for her, jeopardizing her designer store at a time when money would be critically important.

I repeatedly advised Georgia to consult a lawyer, even providing her with the names and addresses of several trustworthy attorneys. She has not followed through. Today she remains married to Goran, alone in her heart and utterly unhappy. She tells me she is waiting for her son to turn eighteen to initiate a divorce. I do not believe her for a moment. I do not think she does, either.

The many stories I have shared demonstrate the important issues that keep high-achieving women imprisoned in destructive relationships. Some may experience one or two of these problems while others must deal with the entire gamut. Because of the attention given to lack of money, careers, and education as factors in keeping women captive, too little attention is paid to the fact that financial independence, education, and cleverness are often not enough to pull us out of bad relationships. These things can even increase the difficulty of making a clean break. And for some of us, the origin of our ills has more to do with conditioning that establishes us on a parallel-track existence, combined with the factors other abused women also experience.

I offer all the above as an explanation, but not as an excuse. We abused women cannot discount our own roles in sustaining unstable relationships. Since it takes two willing partners to prolong a union, it is necessary for us to look deep and hard at our own contributions to our failed marriages. In order to break free of the dangerous cycle of denial, acceptance, and self-pity, we must acknowledge how and why we accept verbal, emotional, and sometimes physical abuse.

CHAPTER 5

The Anatomy of Failure

ONCE WE ARE OUT of a situation, it is often possible to see clearly what we were unable to see while living in it. I would add that neither do we listen until we are ready to listen. Even though Anna, my secretary, had spoken to me numerous times about the issues in my marriage, I had refused to accept what she had observed. Living in denial and refusing to acknowledge the truth or to listen to reason was my maladaptive coping mechanism for survival when admitting my problems would have hurt too much. A romantic relationship is a partnership. After an introspective analysis of my behavior during my marriage, I came to the difficult conclusion that my actions, or lack of action, significantly contributed to the failure of my relationship.

How? That proved a hard question for me to ask, and an even harder one to answer. It took me years to even admit I shared responsibility. Most of the women who participated in my forum exhibited similar maladaptive behaviors and denial.

Where Did I Go Wrong?

My intentions in my marriage were good. My actions were always meant to support our relationship. Given that my wedding vows had stipulated "in good times and in bad," I thought I had to make the marriage work at all costs. Now, looking back, I see that my most defective coping mechanism was flawed logic. This is ironic, since I am a rational person who applies a straightforward formula to all matters apart from my marriage. If I were contemplating a new job, I would create a scale, allotting points to each factor. How important is it to have freedom at work? How does the pay compare with my current job? How safe is the place where I would have to move? How close is that place to good schools for my kids? In my first marriage, I misused reason to create a system of faulty logic that justified my husband's shortcomings and validated my staying in our dysfunctional relationship.

I would say to myself, as long as he does not drink, as long as he does not cheat, as long as he is good with the kids, as long as he does not strike me, it is okay if he has frequent angry spells and insults me. It is okay that he does not often work because I make enough for both of us. I convinced myself that there was no such thing as a perfect partner, even when I was constantly fearful of his next bout of fury, even when he would become remote and refuse to talk to me for days. I did not understand that my husband's behavior bore all the markers for emotional abuse, reinforcing my low self-esteem. I did not understand that my reaction bore all the markers of codependency. Instead of holding him to account, I would wonder what I had done wrong, yet again.

It took years for me to realize that it was not okay for him to call me names. It was not okay for him to rant at me so often. It was not okay for him to give me the silent treatment. It was not okay that I was feeling miserable all the time. This technique of twisted rationalization—of making the illogical appear logical—was used by most of the other women in this book. It was the foundation of our denial. We told ourselves that nothing was wrong or that what we experienced was not such a big deal compared to what other people suffer in their lives. Repression allowed us to bury everything that hurt us deep into our subconscious. The fact that our abuse was long-term created a process of adaptation in which our grief became normal to us.

Some of us contributed to the unhealthy state of our relationships by constantly stroking our husbands' egos. I, for example, would praise him for minor household chores while downplaying his refusal to get up early enough to help me in the morning with the kids. Because I always felt he needed cheering up, I would magnify the importance of any paid job he happened to get, ignoring the fact that I had done all his paperwork, including obtaining any license or permits that were required. In retrospect, I see that I was also validating myself for being with him, and for having chosen him as a life partner. In any relationship, praising worthy behavior is a positive, but when it is used to embellish destructive behavior, it is a negative.

Not only did I inflate my husband's ego, but I also made his issues my own. If he had a problem with his job, his family, or his friends, I was the solver, the savior, the rescuer. We also had a twisted financial exchange. While it was up to me to pay all our bills, most of the spending was up to him. Like several of the other women I interviewed, I was a "pleaser," deriving joy from providing my husband with cars and expensive electronic equipment, none of which he shared with me. I shouldered most of the household and childcare duties, leaving only basic maintenance to him, like shoveling snow, cutting grass, and shopping for groceries. As well as handling complex financial matters, I also did the simplest financial chores such as going to the bank and organizing receipts.

My excuse? I did not want to wait for him to complete tasks, or to admit to his mistakes when he messed up. My husband enjoyed a state of comfortable inertia while I dealt with almost everything, and he took advantage of this arrangement. Truly, I was an enabler. I positioned myself as his ever-present crutch to lean upon and his safety net if he should fall. The bitter truth is that I had married a weak man, and I made him even weaker and less able to fend for himself. Several women in my forum echoed this admission.

Perpetual hope also contributes to the tapestry of flaws in many bad relationships. We always hoped our situation would improve. We believed our soft approach would help our partner to see the error of his ways and ultimately change his behavior. We dreamt that time would make our relationship easier, that we would grow as a couple. We fell into this trap because we did, in fact, experience good times amid the bad ones. We felt temporary optimism whenever we shared special or significant family events, such as graduations, promotions, illnesses, and losses through death. These fleeting moments of mutual support or celebration seemed to strengthen our relationship. Then, all too soon, reality set in and we resumed the vicious cycle of disappointment and hope.

As Loretta, a corporate executive, said during our forum: "Girls, think about it. All of us have described how much we loved our husbands, but no one has mentioned whether they loved us."

Her statement hit home. We had been consumed with loving them, with the "bad boy" factor often playing a role. While most of us had been brought up conservatively, with little exposure to dating, our partners had inhabited a wilder world of drinking and partying. Like Johnny, many were endowed with good looks and muscular physiques, which made them attractive to other women and gave us a rush over the fact that we had been chosen. With Loretta, passionate sex had also been a big turn-on, until the relationship with her "bad boy" suddenly soured.

THE ANATOMY OF FAILURE

Helen

Luckily, some high-achieving women do learn to set boundaries, making their relationships healthier. Since Helen and George were neighbors, I witnessed their evolution. George was a builder of expensive country homes, which had been featured in newspapers and magazines. Helen, who had a business degree, worked part-time as his company's bookkeeper while raising their two daughters and one son. George was an alcoholic. On construction sites, he would drink a beer here and there. During long meetings with customers, he would put hard liquor into his coffee. He drank during dinner, at social events, and especially over the weekend. Without this daily intake, George experienced withdrawal symptoms.

Helen described George as "a happy drunk in his own world." However, when he was not giddy he was remote, belligerent, and sometimes violent, throwing furniture and other objects. He had also hit Helen on a couple of occasions. Even during the rare times when George was sober, he would call Helen names and be abrupt, rude, and uncaring.

Helen had grown up with an alcoholic father. She had often witnessed her father's angry drunken spells and her mother's reaction to them. Now, as an adult married to a drunk, she was on a path similar to her mother's. She worried when George was out drinking. If he did not return home, she searched for him in the bars he frequented. She felt sorry for him when he cried after his abusive drunken spells, while simultaneously feeling angry at him for repeating the same behaviors.

At last, in despair, and with my encouragement, Helen visited a counselor. Through surreptitious therapy sessions, she started to understand what codependency was and how she was contributing to her own misfortune by enabling George's behavior. For change to occur, Helen had to learn to love and value herself, as well as to define boundaries for George. It was a long and painful process, but Helen made substantial progress, supported by her three adult children who sometimes visited the counselor with her.

One afternoon, Helen told George she wanted to talk. She did not inform him that this was to be an intervention about his substance abuse. Their children were present. George was taken by surprise. He could not believe his ears when his quiet and subdued wife informed him she had visited a lawyer and was prepared to divorce him if he did not stop drinking. The children backed Helen up by telling their father they had advised her to do this and collectively vowing to disown him if he did not acquiesce to the conditions laid out by the family. One of George's daughters made these terms specific by telling him he was unwelcome at her engagement party.

After years of denial, George received an ultimatum that cornered him. Yet, for the intervention to work, the desire for rehabilitation had to come from within himself. This was George's deciding moment. He realized he had too much to lose if he did not accept his family's terms. He checked himself in to a rehabilitation clinic, joined Alcoholics Anonymous, and managed to overcome his addiction over the course of two years, suffering only one relapse. Helen joined Al-Anon, a support organization for family members of alcoholics. Ten years later, George is still sober and the couple has sustained their relationship with the continuing help of AA and Al-Anon.

Unfortunately, happy endings like this seem to be an exception. Helen first had to realize how she had contributed to her husband's behavior by tolerating it, feeling sorry for him, and putting his needs above her own. She was a key player who had to change herself before she could set terms for her husband to change. In this, she was fortunate to have the support of a wise counselor, understanding children, along with a husband capable of rising to a very difficult challenge.

Gordana

The compulsion to nurture one's partner, and to cater to his will, seems to be the Achilles' heel of many women, at the expense of our own emotional, physical, and financial well-being. Gordana came to Canada with her husband, Andrei, during the 1990s turmoil caused by the breakup of Yugoslavia. She was a very attractive woman, in her early forties, warm and chatty, with an exceptional physique due to regular gym work. Though Gordana was a university graduate, like so many immigrants she had had to accept part-time retail work that underused her capabilities and training.

Andrei, who was twice Gordana's size, was a heavy-equipment operator in construction. They had a son—their pride and joy who excelled both academically and in sports. My second husband and I sometimes met Gordana and Andrei on Sundays at our local coffee shop where we would chat. Though these were infrequent encounters, I came to know Gordana as a positive person, always giggling and ready to tell a funny joke. Andrei was also good company, half of the time. During his bad moods, he seemed withdrawn, cynical, and angry at the world. On those occasions, we exchanged few words with him, although Gordana always found time to visit our table.

Given Andrei's wild fluctuations between euphoria and depression, I suspected he had a bipolar disorder. Gordana arrived a little late to my women's forum because she had been working that Saturday and listened quietly to all of our stories. She did not contribute until near the end, when a couple of women talked about their attraction to "bad boys" who always caused them serious grief.

"Bad boys?" commented Gordana. "I have had one all my life. But my love for my bad boy is long gone, dead, never to return."

I was taken aback, because she and Andrei had always seemed affectionate, despite his mood swings. Two days later, I received a frantic call at my office from Gordana.

"Angela, please, I need to talk to you."

That evening, we met again at our coffee shop. After catching her breath, Gordana poured out her story. It contained all the familiar elements of the other shared forum stories.

Gordana was raised in a strict, religious family, which firmly believed in the sanctity of marriage. Partly because of her lack of dating experience, she had been attracted to Andrei, whose education was much less than her own. For twenty years, she had dealt with his mood swings, sudden spells of anger, emotional and physical aggression, grandiose plans when he was "too happy," suicidal ideations when he was depressed. Andrei had stubbornly refused to see a doctor, relying instead on reality-evading mechanisms such as drugs and booze. As the recipient of Andrei's pathological jealousy, Gordana became his servant, sex object, cushion, and punching bag. She catered to his needs, prepared his meals, gave him sex on command, and even sold her land back in Europe to bail him out of debt when a business he started in Canada failed.

In return, Andrei mocked and undermined Gordana. When she landed her first retail job, he predicted that she would not last more than two weeks. Not only did she last but she had also found a second part-time job. In public, Gordana continued to praise Andrei, minimizing his shortcomings, elevating his ego, and hiding behind the facade of a contented woman. Now, Gordana confessed that the forum at my home had allowed her to realize her marriage was a sham. Encouraged by the other women, she had surprised herself by overcoming her family's taboos to disclose, for the first time, that she was not in love with her husband and that their marriage was in peril.

"Something happened to me that night," Gordana confessed, still shaking her head in disbelief.

We discussed counseling and divorce, but Gordana seemed too frightened, too emotionally weak, and too insecure to take action.

I did not think she would terminate her marriage anytime soon, because she seemed greatly preoccupied with how Andrei would suffer if she left him. Given his volatile temperament, I also worried that walking out might put her in danger.

That forum at my home was the beginning of a long, convoluted journey for Gordana, a courageous first step, with more to come. As both my marriage and Gordana's demonstrate, we abused woman play a key role in our entrapment, partly because of tendencies bestowed by nature. However, the biological factors that make us nurturers, listeners, pleasers, rescuers, team players, and nonconfrontational punching bags do not force us to become lifelong victims. In the words of scientists Scott Langevin and Karl Kelsey, "Our DNA does not fully dictate our destiny."[30]

CHAPTER 6

Ending One Path, Starting Another

O N A LOVELY SPRING EVENING in the late 1990s, as Sophia and I sipped Greek coffee on the deck of my Toronto home, we had good reason to take stock of our lives. It had been five years since my divorce and two since Sophia's. We were reminiscing about the events that released us from our mental inertia, allowing us to escape our miserable lives. I was recalling my long period of preparation, during which I acquainted myself with my inner woman, partly by reinventing my outer woman. This process had included NordicTrack workouts, aerobic line dancing, and then rewarding myself with a stylish new wardrobe.

In 1993, while I was still married but preparing for flight, I had received a payoff for this difficult makeover when I returned to Greece to visit my sister's family. Just before this ten-day trip, my grade-twelve classmate, Lia, told me she would throw a welcoming party for as many of our former classmates as she could reach. Since our high-school graduation twenty-three years ago, I had all but vanished, keeping in touch with no one. Lia's party would be a big event for me. Many of my female classmates had been objects of my teenaged envy, and my memory of their beauty had haunted me throughout my adult life.

For the reunion, I put on a black designer dress paired with black high heels. My heart was pounding as I arrived at our rendezvous—a Greek tavern in a cozy suburb of Athens. I was met with loud welcoming shouts, hugs, and kisses from twenty men and women, all in their early forties. The girls touched my hair and made me turn around a few times so they could see "the moth that turned into a butterfly." The compliments of the Greek men were typically less poetic, referring to certain prominent body parts. One classmate, now a well-known architect, exclaimed, "Man! I've never seen a woman turn into such a kick-ass babe at forty."

I was equally startled but for opposite reasons. I could not believe how the women who had established my ideals of beauty had changed. One female classmate who had won many athletic trophies now appeared short and out of shape. A popular volleyball player looked like she had not been near a court for many years. The girl with the long, wavy black hair was unattractively skinny, with a short spiky do and heavy makeup covering acne scars.

Lia, who hosted the party, and our classmate, Katerina, had made it through the years quite unscathed. As mature working women with kids and husbands, time had actually enhanced their natural beauty. Their skin glowed, with few wrinkles, and their bodies were toned. They dressed with taste and wore discreet makeup. Everything about them exuded care and elegance. Their secret? They were the only two who regularly trained at the gym or played outdoor sports.

As for the men, only vegetarian Andreas and my architect friend seemed in decent shape. Most of the others appeared deconditioned, with prominent bellies and hair that was turning gray or balding. The Tom Cruise kind of guy on whom most of us had had a crush failed to show. Now a banker, I was told he avoided social gatherings and now weighed over 350 pounds. My Greek visit strengthened my conviction that physical exercise was a key to health and beauty. It had become second nature to me since the early 1990s when Johnny's disrespect, antagonism, and constant putdowns had given me drive.

Another revelation was how differently my classmates remembered me in comparison to how I thought they had perceived me. The girls, who had made me cringe with jealousy those many years ago, now confessed that they had actually been envious of me and were even more so now. A few men told me they had had crushes on me but had not dared approach me given my condescending attitude—all a facade, of course, to cover my insecurity.

How could I have been so wrong about my classmates' feelings all these years? How could my perceptions have been so different, and why?

A distorted interpretation of reality is common during our teenage years, and some of us hold on to that view abnormally long, perhaps even indefinitely. By providing another mirror, the reunion allowed me to see my former self in a positive light through the eyes of my classmates.

Another push in my evolution came three years later when beautiful Katerina, who seemed to be the epitome of health and fitness, found out she had advanced ovarian cancer. Katerina was the mother of two daughters, a high-ranking administrator in a Greek shipping company, and a gym-and-nutrition freak who trained four to five times a week and who ran marathons. When she sought medical advice for a lingering pelvic pain, it was too late. She underwent chemotherapy, radiation, and surgery, but nonetheless died of cancer.

Katerina's illness and death, so close to my sister Pari's near-fatal illness, hit me hard. It was also one of those defining events that caused me to look deeper into my life, leading me to the dreadful conclusion that, while my professional self had done well, my personal self had failed. The prospect of living a stagnant, resentful life with a partner I no longer loved or respected shook me to the bone.

Other Discovery Moments

Several women in my forum described similar turning points, eureka events that caused them to begin the termination of their unhealthy relationship. For Rosa, this happened when her drug-addicted husband asked her son's friends for money to facilitate his habit. The sheer desperation of that act signaled the end of their marriage.

For Marina, a certified general accountant, all hell broke loose when she discovered hidden phone bills that proved, beyond a shred of doubt, that her husband was a sex addict, hooked on escort and prostitution services at three hundred dollars a pop. Suddenly, she had an explanation for his emotional withdrawal, his huge credit-card debts, and the sexually transmitted infections he had passed on to her.

Though the decay in Eva's marriage had been apparent for years, it was not until she discovered her husband's gambling problem, which lost him thousands of hard-earned household dollars on the green table, that she decided to pack up. A high-ranking university administrator and a vibrant, good-looking woman of Scottish heritage, Eva had, at eighteen, married Mark, who had less education and a highly dysfunctional upbringing. As her neighbor for many years, I witnessed one of her continuing problems: Mark's relatives would take over their home every weekend, forcing her to entertain and provide meals. Though Mark jealously opposed Eva's desire to pursue further university studies, she continued to stroke his ego, praising his little successes to raise his self-esteem, a behavior all too familiar to me. Under Mark's barrage of criticisms about her perceived imperfections, she had shut down emotionally until she found those gambling debts. While Mark was in Las Vegas on a four-day binge, she paid all of their household bills, rented a truck, and moved with her children to her parents' basement apartment. Mark was infuriated on returning to a partially empty house, less because Eva had left with the kids but because she had taken some of his favorite pieces of furniture.

Wife Abandonment Syndrome

Rosa, Marina, and Eva, all forum women, had watched their marriages slowly deteriorate until they became untenable. However, sometimes it is the high-achieving woman who is blindsided by her partner's sudden, unexpected departure. Loretta, a beautiful, intelligent, adventure-craving Maritimer, fell in love in her twenties with a tall, handsome, muscular sailor. During their passionate relationship, he seemed to transform from a quintessential bad boy into a loving and caring spouse whom Loretta called her "white knight." When they had a child, Loretta, a radiology technologist, felt she was living her dream, never suspecting that her white knight, on his many service trips, was frequenting bars, drinking, fighting, gambling, and womanizing. At our forum, Loretta vividly recalled coming home from the hospital one December 12 carrying their second daughter. Twelve days later, her white knight gave her the worst Christmas Eve present imaginable. He announced he was leaving her for another woman. He packed his bags and vanished from Loretta's life, leaving her to care for their two babies.

Loretta was devastated. Thankfully, her mother flew in from the Maritimes to support her while she pieced together her broken heart and healed her shriveled pride. Today, Loretta is a highly successful businesswoman, married to a man who is "100 percent good" and who helped her to raise her two wonderful daughters. The unstoppable attitude that had propelled Loretta's career helped her survive her marital humiliation.

Loretta is an example of Wife Abandonment Syndrome (WAS), a term coined by Montreal social worker Vikki Stark in her 2010 book *Runaway Husbands* to describe spouses who abruptly leave without ever expressing their unhappiness. In Stark's own case, she had just told her husband of twenty-one years that she had bought fish for dinner, when he announced, "I can't do this anymore."

It took Stark a minute to realize her husband was talking about their marriage, not about the fish. After he pulled his vanishing act, she went through what she described as "an emotional concussion." As part of her recovery, she researched what she labeled Wife Abandonment Syndrome, wrote her book, set up a website, and was contacted by hundreds of other women with similar stories to share.

The Long, Winding Road of Separation and Divorce

For most women, the transition out of a bad relationship is a slow, gradual, grim reality with many steps and stages. We drag our feet through the difficult process of admitting the relationship is not working, make efforts to repair it, and finally conclude it cannot be fixed. Even after I experienced a revelation about my own situation, I found myself constantly taking two steps forward and one back. This seemed necessary and unavoidable. Most of us continue to be plagued by intense, conflicted feelings, leading to a roller coaster of emotions. We agonize over how to walk away, and then have to endure legal and emotional battles while trying to mitigate the impact on our children. We question whether our decision was the right one, we fear future regret, we despair over the years we've lost, and we panic about facing the future alone.

Our convoluted path does not end with the divorce. Once we are out of the relationship, we face a lengthy process of repair. My biggest problem was the emotional damage to my kids, along with needing to recover financially. My temporary solution was to keep my brain busy by plunging into work. I told myself I would not think about anything else until I had healed.

Rosa's period of emotional recovery was made more difficult when she found her ex was already dating another woman. After leaving her gambling husband, Eva endured many years of social isolation, interacting only with her kids and her immediate family, while putting all of her energy into her job. Marina, who discovered her husband was a sex addict, overcame her depression by dealing hands-on with her accountants, lawyers, and bankers to salvage her personal fortune. "I brought all my business skills into what became a job," she said, "and I am very good at completing jobs." She blames today's occasional bouts of sadness on her one regret: "I wasted so many years."

I gave Marina a wonderful piece of advice that I had received: "Spend only 5 percent of your energy grieving the past, and 95 percent working on the present to improve your future." Unfortunately, some women just cannot make it that far.

Marina continued to go back and forth with her spouse, while he escalated his emotional abuse to physical violence. Despite calls from me and from other friends urging her to leave this dangerous situation, Marina would not listen. Last I heard, she had lost her job because of underperformance and had removed herself from all contact.

Martha, my children's Greek teacher, has never lost her bitterness over having been abandoned by her lazy, cheating husband. I learned the story of Dianne, a legal secretary, from one of the women who participated in my forum. After she had moved out of a ten-year dysfunctional relationship with full custody of her two-year-old son, she sought comfort in a series of failed relationships. The lesson she learned? "Don't enter a relationship to heal, but when you are healed."

Lisa, a very attractive patient of mine with Southern European roots, celebrated her divorce with a few plastic surgeries (facelift, breast augmentation, tummy tuck). Though they made her look at least fifteen years younger, they did not heal her broken heart. She began making the rounds of bars and night clubs, "being a slut," as she described it.

Melody, a Canadian-born family physician whose parents came from Japan, forged her way out of an abusive marriage to another doctor because of her intense desire for a new partner. She joined a gym, started dance lessons, and rose through the ranks of her department. After she left my hospital to become chief of family practice at another institution, I assumed everything was going exceptionally well for her. That is, until I encountered her four years later at a professional meeting. At first, I did not recognize her. She had obviously not been taking care of herself. When I greeted Melody, her eyes slipped right past me as if she did not want to talk. I did not dare ask how she was doing. It seemed obvious.

The Financial Cost of Spousal Abuse

A report by the Justice Department of Canada, obtained in 2012 by the Canadian Press under the Access to Information Act, concluded, "Spousal violence is a widespread and unfortunate social reality that has an effect on all Canadians."[31] "Spouse" in this report included married, common-law, separated, same-sex, and divorced partners. This violence was estimated to cost Canadian society at least $7.4 billion a year. In almost fifty thousand cases of spousal violence reported to police in 2009, some 80 percent involved female victims. These cases included sixty-five homicides, forty-nine of them women. The conservatively calculated $7.4 billion estimate included everything from bills for prosecutions and emergency-room visits to personal expenses such as relocation to escape harassment. Only 7 percent of the costs were borne by Canada's justice system, which included legal aid. Third parties (employers, social-service agencies) picked up 12 percent. The victims bore roughly 80 percent, amounting to some $6 billion.

In the United States, the costs of domestic abuse as manifested in health care spending, criminal behavior, and loss of labor market productivity is estimated at $55 billion a year.[32] Sixty-six percent of victims of domestic violence indicate that their ability to work is affected by the violence, and half of battered women who are employed are harassed at work by their abusive partners.[33] Of course, money is not the primary concern when it comes to domestic abuse but statistics like these show that everyone in society has a stake in seeing it disappear.

CHAPTER 7

Recovery: Surviving, Then Thriving

ONCE A WOMAN DECIDES to leave a bad relationship, she will have many issues to tackle and many wounds to heal. One crucial decision she will make early on is getting the right legal advice. When I started my divorce process, I went to the lawyer who had handled my real-estate purchases. He realized my breakup would be "no walk in the park" and advised me to seek a legal expert who specialized in family law. After checking the internet, I chose a firm that seemed to specialize in difficult divorces and made an appointment to see one of their female partners. My sister Pari, who was visiting once again, accompanied me.

As soon I began telling my story, I could see from the doubt in the lawyer's eyes that she did not believe me. Apparently, she could not connect the well-published, well-known physician, whom she had in turn researched on the internet, with the person in front of her, unable to complete a sentence about her terrorized kids or her frightened calls to the police without dissolving into tears. The lawyer's consoling words, spoken with authority, sounded like scripted advice to any distraught woman.

Despite that uncertain beginning, my lawyer became my counselor as she navigated me, slowly, through a draining year-long legal obstacle course. It involved court orders to oblige the sale of the matrimonial home and the division of assets, including household items. Then came custodial arrangements, also bitterly contested. My hard-earned lesson is that contested divorces do require lawyers with expertise in family law and that these lawyers are costly.

In retrospect, I would have liked my lawyer to have taken a more aggressive approach to resolving my issues. I also came to reject her referrals to "counselors" whose highly ineffective presence in the lives of myself and my children were a frustrating waste of time and money. Some people may have had better experiences with counselors, but they did not work at all for me. Since my divorce, the province of Ontario has established rules for mandatory mediation proceedings, which have the potential to avoid expensive legal councils and courtroom procedures.

Finances

When I finally escaped my relationship of almost three decades, I owned nothing except debts to the taxman and my lawyers. I also had to pay alimony for two and a half years. In fact, both Johnny and I walked away with very little, after watching all we had disappear into the hands of lawyers, mediators, counselors, and a slow and incompetent legal system.

Fortunately, I had a career that allowed me to rebuild my finances over time, while Johnny never managed to stay afloat. On his own, he was lost, overwhelmed by medical issues and by living expenses. Through his own stubbornness, he was left with nothing besides short-term alimony and a lifelong grudge, fueled by anger and hatred that he still harbors twenty-four years later because of "his life that I took away."

Any woman in my position will end her legal separation with significant bills, including alimony, or at least a hefty loss from the division of assets. If the matrimonial house was sold, she will have to relocate herself and her kids. Based on the experiences of the high-achieving women I spoke to, her ex will likely have left unpaid bills and unfulfilled obligations to deal with. Most of the successful career women I know had either the lion's share of joint custody or the "whole lion," as I did, which entails serious financial obligations. Even if custody is shared, I have heard of many drawn-out court battles because an ex failed to pay child support.

Our Kids and the New World

The well-being of our kids is a substantial issue, especially when they are young and dependent and when the divorce is acrimonious. Though I concentrated on giving my sons as normal a life as possible, they retained vivid memories of unpleasant events that even I had repressed and that marked them for a long time.

My ex-husband disappeared from my sons' lives for years, appearing only intermittently to grieve what he considered an unjust separation and to complain about how badly I had made him feel.

Now in their early thirties, my sons are able to set boundaries for their father. First and foremost, he is never to talk about the divorce, making their relationship more pleasant and meaningful. As a footnote, I should state that I continued in the early years after the divorce to help my ex-husband through some hard times, functioning as a shadow behind my boys to meet some of his financial needs without his ever knowing. I could not bear to see my sons suffer over the stark difference between the lifestyles of the two people who brought them into this world. Now that they are financially independent, they bear the brunt of their father's financial dependency.

Sophia's ex-husband failed to create a post-divorce relationship with his daughters, but thanks to Sophia's unconditional love, the girls grew into independent young ladies who adore their mother (their "rock"). Both Sophia and I were relatively lucky with our children, but some kids are permanently traumatized, both from the dysfunctional marriage and from the divorce.

Jane, a manager of a string of medical laboratories, faced many issues while raising her daughter and two sons. During long years of marital discord, her cheating husband had emotionally abused the children as well as Jane. After their ugly, prolonged, and heavily contested divorce, he withheld tuition fees that he could easily have afforded. He would agree to take the kids but then refuse to do so, disappointing them and forcing Jane to cancel her holidays. When he remarried, he failed to inform the children until much later.

Jane's resilient daughter ended up in a healthy, happy relationship, but her boys experimented with drugs, were expelled for fighting in class, and almost failed to finish high school. One fell into a deep depression, requiring hospitalization. Many years later, they still carry emotional scars.

Is there such a thing as a "family bill of breakup rights?" Maybe there should be. I suggest the following:

1. Explain to the kids that it's not their fault that their parents are moving in different directions, and that they will continue to be loved and cherished by both mother and father.
2. Make formal custody arrangements based on the needs and well-being of the children, factoring in each parent's ability to assist with schoolwork, with transportation to school and to after-school activities, and so on.

3. Establish terms, including boundaries, on how to handle family occasions, graduations, birthdays, and holidays.
4. Establish reasonable access for relationships with grandparents.
5. Never, ever use the kids as depositories of parental anger or sorrow, including badmouthing or asking them to spy on the ex-spouse.

Of course, it takes two to make a deal. If the rules are upheld by only one parent, the damage to the kids may be unavoidable. However, when they themselves are old enough, knowing the rules may help them to become effective in establishing fairness and boundaries with both parents, as happened with my two sons.

On Being Single Again

Often we remember broken relationships in the same way we remember the dead. Painful memories recede, while the good moments become enhanced, skewing our reality. Social gatherings, which we must now attend alone, may trigger sorrow. We may even turn down invitations, to avoid mingling in the world of couples. While anger or grieving are normal reactions to the loss of a relationship and parts of our social circle, if unduly protracted, they can become pathological, perhaps requiring therapeutic help to break the pattern.

I have to admit that confronting the couples' world really bothered me. I used to mull this over with my neighbor, Eva, the university administrator who left her gambler husband at almost the same time as I left mine. Because we had entered long-term relationships when naive, inexperienced, and under twenty, we diagnosed ourselves as having an "attachment handicap." We had no pattern for discovering enjoyment on our own. We did not even know what it was like to go out with a group of girlfriends. I found myself becoming jealous of single women who were able to enjoy solitary activities, such as gardening, golfing, seeing films, or solo dining. Instead, I immersed myself in my work, socializing only with my sons.

This pattern began to change when I formed a long-distance relationship for a couple of years with a colleague. We talked daily on the phone, but only saw each other every couple of months. Nevertheless, this relationship shifted my "singleness" enough that I began to enjoy other people's company over the many weekends that my companion was not around.

While Eva's period of solitude lasted longer, she was much more successful in training herself to enjoy her own company. She began by spending time at her parents' cottage, sometimes with her kids, sometimes alone. After she acquired her boating license, she was able to navigate the family sailboat by herself. Sophia also spent years in "romantic isolation," as she called it, while she healed her wounds.

Michelle, the doctor and volunteer sports coach, raised another issue many women face after leaving abusive relationships: lack of trust. She pointed at the fifteen-foot ceiling of the conference center where we were chatting. "I have built a wall that tall to keep men out." Afraid of another failure, Michelle suspected that anyone who approached her was a predator, like her husband, who had seen her as "his golden goose." The marital failures of her two career-oriented sisters, who had also married young, reinforced this idea. After eight years of withdrawal, Michelle met a man completely outside her professional environment while she was coaching. He approached her gently, slowly, and methodically, and after years of friendship, she lowered her defenses. Today, Michelle and her new partner share a home, a love of sports, and an excitingly active life. Because he had understood Michelle's need to heal, he gradually helped her to rebuild trust, opening windows in her heart and her mind.

When I asked Michelle if it had been difficult to connect with someone outside her professional environment, she replied:

"Absolutely not. For me, that's the secret of our success. We share our separate pursuits with equal passion."

Some high-achieving women require therapy to understand why their marriages went wrong, as well as to learn to accept and to love themselves. I never sought professional help during my hard years or the divorce process. It was only after my divorce that I consulted Tony, who read some of this book's original drafts and helped me to analyze, in retrospect, what had happened to me. Of course, Anna, my secretary and friend, was in her own way a kind of therapist to me, as well. Later, I found the experiences of divorced women extremely beneficial. I enjoyed their non-judgmental camaraderie, and the solidarity created by our frank conversations. These served as a two-way mirror while we sought answers, understanding, consolation, and healing.

The Payoff

I have talked at length about the difficulties of moving on after a bad marriage, separation, and divorce. Now let us look at the payoff: freedom to embrace new interests, to visit new places, to pursue more education or a different career, to create new businesses, to become our own bosses, to own our decision-making, to be the captains of our ships, to find new friends, and to make peace with ourselves.

For most of us, the hard lessons we have learned last a lifetime. Once we truly understand where we have been and define our goals, there is much less possibility of falling into another abusive relationship. Like Michelle, some of us may go overboard in the opposite direction: scrutinizing a new partner's every word and interpreting every argument as abuse. This paranoia can be as much a threat to forming a new relationship as an ex-alcoholic's seeing addiction in every friend's glass of beer. I must confess that, at times, I have been unable to discriminate a spat from emotional abuse. Most of us, however, learn to strike a balance. We understand that lack of trust of others really reflects a lack of trust of ourselves. We go on to create new partnerships, or remain contentedly unattached, cherishing our immense freedom and independence.

It took two divorces before Tatiana, my aesthetician from Russia, was able to describe her life as "absolutely beautiful." I have known her for over twenty years, and will continue to visit the same spa just to be her client. She is a tall, attractive redhead, with a firm body, glowing skin, and two kids in university. Tatiana's first marriage lasted three years; both partners were only twenty. Her second lasted nineteen years, until she walked out on a man she described as "badmouthing, lazy, and extremely negative." Later, when she sometimes bumped into him at her kids' high-school graduations, she learned he was as negative as ever: "bad country, bad people, bad life." Yet when she spoke about him, her voice never resonated with either anger or sorrow.

I asked Tatiana, "So, what is going on in your life today? Are you seeing anyone?"

"Oh yes," she said. "We met shortly after my last divorce, and we have been together four years."

"Are you thinking of marrying again?"

"Are you kidding me? Why? He lives in his own place, we meet often, have a nice dinner, go places together, then head back to our own homes and our separate lives. I do not want to serve or clean for any man anymore. I do not need anyone to support me or my kids. I own my home, and I own my life. I tell you, Angela, my life at fifty is the best it has ever been!"

It may have been hard, it may have been bumpy, it may have been long, but most of the women I spoke to managed to rebuild their lives, to achieve equilibrium, and to capture happiness in one form or another. For women in troubled relationships, it is most important to realize there is life beyond the fear, the anxiety, the depression, and the problem-solving of ending a bad union.

CHAPTER 8

Dating Again

I GREW UP KNOWING HOW Greek men felt about women—or, at least, how they did forty years ago when I left my homeland. Men of my father's generation, and of my own, believed the job of women was to serve them (at home and in bed) while their job was to protect us. At the same time, I have to credit my autocratic father for the freedom to pursue my studies—a duality in his personality that made my upbringing as a girl different from the norm. To this day, I can remember the hours he spent by my side, silently watching while I studied into the night or focused on writing a physiology book. At the same time, it was utterly unacceptable for me to criticize him for not taking his dishes to the sink or otherwise helping out around our home. He also constricted my innate sense of femaleness by dictating a very conservative style of dress and restricting my social life. Because my sister found it easier to conform to family demands, the poor girl ended up with more chores than me; my parents always told her, "Angela is busy studying." Pari has never let me forget this.

Social Evolution

I had little contact with my homeland, after leaving for Canada, until the early 1990s when I began to attend periodic classmate reunions. In the summer of 2000, a few years after my divorce, I was with a group of twenty, all of us in our mid-forties, equally divided between men and women. We were enjoying a gorgeous summer evening, in a cafeteria in a trendy seaside suburb of Athens, when someone asked me about my work. As I excitedly described one of my projects, which was studying the brain activity of patients with chronic pain, a male engineer interrupted me.

"You are too smart!" he said. "With all that scientific shit in your head, do you think you are going to find a man? Dream on! You won't even find a male dog."

I was stunned, and I was not the only one. His statement provoked an animated discussion. The women were offended by what they intuited as this engineer's inferiority complex, leading to his fear of women who openly displayed intelligence and sexuality. Despite the fact that several men took his side, I realized that a social evolution had occurred in Greece since I had left. All of the women in that gathering were financially independent teachers, social workers, bank managers, or business owners. All had ongoing careers, except for a judge who had opted for early retirement to look after her kids. Six of the ten women (including me) were divorced. All six had initiated their divorces, with abuse and exploitation as common reasons, demonstrating that escape from entrapment was now a reality, at least in the capital of Greece.

By contrast, all but one of the men in our group were married, mostly to stay-at-home wives. The exception was a bachelor, who was contemplating marrying his longtime girlfriend. Here was a clear split: educated working women were more likely to be single than women who had opted to stay home. While I cannot claim our group was an accurate barometer of modern Greece, it seemed that my female peers, who had conquered the boardroom, had paid the price of trouble in the bedroom. On the plus side, the old Greek assumptions that "divorce does not happen in good families" and "divorce is a woman's shame" were giving way to more modern, equitable ones even in this Old World society.

I shared my Greek experience with Sophia shortly after my return to Toronto. Since her southern Italian Catholic culture and mine were so similar, my story resonated with her. Fresh from her own divorce, she was finding the single world scary. The Toronto bar scene made her uncomfortable, and her social environment was limited. She wanted male companionship and was discouraged about finding it. Since I had the same desire, I suggested: "Why don't we join a reputable dating agency? Plenty of them match single professional women with suitable partners."

Sophia's jaw dropped. Though the idea was also out of character for me, we decided we had nothing to lose by giving it a try. Magazine and television advertisements hailing the success of these commercial matchmakers gave us confidence, as did our assumption that the improved gender equality in North American workplaces would also mean gender equality in dating.

Sophia and I put our logical brains to work and came up with a checklist of positive and negative points regarding appearance, intelligence, interests and hobbies, family circumstances, education, profession, and finances, against which we would score the men we met. This plan of action was like the objective ones we used in business and scientific research. We assumed that any agency catering to single professionals would pair us with partners who respected each other's careers and autonomy. We intended to do the choosing, not to be chosen.

Sophia and I joined different dating agencies to compare notes. Though it cost us several thousand dollars apiece, we chose to think of it as an investment. Each of us then created an extensive biography describing our personality, our background, and our interests, as well as describing the qualities we were looking for in a companion. This information would be entered into databases to match us up with suitable partners. Both partners would then be provided with phone numbers to introduce ourselves in cafés or restaurants.

Over six months, Sophia and I embarked on a crash course in dating, easily making up for our limited previous experience. Being well organized, we both kept diaries with meticulous descriptions of the men we met and our interactions with them. We shared every detail to support each other through our different encounters. Despite our bold assumptions, we still possessed lingering fears that our professional success might present an obstacle.

That fear proved well grounded. We repeatedly experienced male attitudes to career women here in Canada like those in Greece. As women in our forties, we belonged to one of the first waves to break through the glass ceiling—the ceiling created by many of our male colleagues.

Larry was a pleasant, wealthy developer a few years older than me. He was elegant and slim, with gray hair and a soft voice. He had come to Canada from Malta at age seven and had been divorced for several years. He was close with his three grown children. Larry and I spent an interesting evening in a restaurant, talking about our professions and our families. When we parted, he promised to call me so that we could meet again. Since I was impressed with his even temper, his gentleness, and his devotion to his children, I was looking forward to another engagement.

Larry did call, a couple of days later, but not to set up another meeting. He said that, while he liked me very much, after some serious thinking, he had decided that I was not for him. I asked why.

"I am sorry," he said (and this is word for word), "but I do not want to live in the shadow of your career, running after you at a hundred miles an hour."

I was surprised and disappointed, while appreciating how transparent he was about his feelings. I thanked Larry for his honesty, and never saw him again.

After a number of fruitless introductions, far from the appropriate matches the agencies guaranteed, I was finally referred to Andrew, a Canadian-born computer consultant who was divorced, an intellectual, a lover of opera, and physically stunning. We met in a posh downtown restaurant, where we engaged in an animated conversation that revealed many common interests. Three days later, when we again met for dinner, Andrew told me how much he had been looking forward to seeing me. He also confided that he was an aspiring fiction writer who had just uploaded a novel to an internet website in the hope of finding a publisher.

I replied that I had just finished a popular science book about pain for which I had a literary agent and a publisher's contract. Andrew's demeanor instantly changed and I did not hear from him for over a week. Finally, he returned my call to say that he had been busy juggling his time "trying to meet several women."

Needless to say, I was disappointed, but I was also baffled. I could not understand his sudden change of heart, except to surmise that he did not like the fact that I had a publisher while he did not.

Meet-and-greet was not going much better for Sophia. She had been paired with men diametrically different to her in interests and lifestyle, some much older and unappealing, and others who were "far too busy to even think of a relationship." She thought her luck might be improving when she was introduced to Mario, an attractive Italian, around her age, with curly gray hair and an eloquent voice. The owner of a safety equipment business, he was also a great ballroom dancer.

At an initial meeting in a coffee shop, Sophia and Mario seemed to hit it off. Since Mario wanted to introduce her to ballroom dancing, they met at a bar in Little Italy that offered couples' lessons.

Sophia again had a good time and they agreed to keep meeting on Fridays for dance lessons. At the end of that first night, Mario gave Sophia a passionate goodnight kiss.

For the next few days, Mario telephoned Sophia every night to chat, letting her know that he was looking forward to seeing her again. On Thursday night, their phone talk went a little deeper. Mario confessed that he was reeling from his bad divorce and was still struggling financially to make ends meet. Sophia commiserated before telling him, by way of encouragement, that she had been in the same situation but had managed to pay off her debts and was now in the process of buying a house.

They said their goodbyes with Sophia still anticipating their dance class the following night. Very, very early on Saturday morning, Sophia called me, choking on tears. She and Mario had danced for two enjoyable hours on Friday evening before Mario announced that he wanted to talk.

"Listen, Sophia," he said loudly, to be heard over the music, "I do not want to see you again. You really do not turn me on."

At first, Sophia thought she had not heard him correctly. She asked him to repeat himself and he did, even more loudly. Sophia was grateful the bar had rotating lights so Mario could not see her flushed face and sudden tears.

"How come?" she managed to whisper. "I thought things were going well—we had good conversations and fun together."

"Yeah, but the issue for me is that you just do not turn me on, so there's no point in seeing you again."

He continued mercilessly, "Besides, you are kind of old for me. Did you know that my previous girlfriend was eighteen?"

Sophia walked out of the place, found her car and drove home. She then lay in bed, numbly staring at the ceiling until four in the morning when she knew I would soon be getting up. Bawling her eyes out, Sophia asked me to help her understand what was going on. I thought it a testament to how comfortable she felt in her own skin that it had never crossed her mind before Mario's brutal comments that he had not found her attractive. Years ago, this encounter would have demolished her. Now she felt only deceived and offended, along with a burning desire to understand the reasoning behind the behavior of Mario and the other Marios we had met—Canadian-born, Southern European, Middle Eastern, South Asian—some mismatches leaving us with laughter, others with wonder, or even sorrow.

I comforted her with what I had concluded: "We are good-looking, interesting, successful, smart woman. This is too much for some men to accept, and they do not know how to handle their emotional discomfort. The only one with enough backbone to tell me the truth was Larry. Andrew walked away when he found I was in the process of publishing a book while he was struggling to achieve a similar goal. As for Mario, the fact you're so much better off financially was probably too much for his big, Italian male ego. His inferiority complex prompted him to sever your relationship in a mean-spirited way. No doubt putting you down felt better to him than admitting his real problem. Who does that remind you of?"

This reference to Sophia's former husband gave her an immediate handle on Mario's behavior. "Wow. I thought women had more social equality here in North America. Guess not," she said wryly.

Other Approaches

After we abandoned the dating agencies, Sophia placed a personal ad in a major newspaper for a weekend, leaving a cellphone number: "Fit, attractive, 5′6″ professional Caucasian woman in early forties who loves travel, music, and romantic encounters, seeks same for serious relationship."

Within hours, she received a phone call. The voice was assertive, with a slight accent Sophia could not identify. Richard said he was a computer consultant in his early fifties who owned his own company. He also described himself as slim, fit, and very tall—almost six feet—divorced, with two adult children. When Sophia asked if he was sure he was a match for the woman she described in her ad, he responded confidently, "Ninety-nine point nine-nine percent—otherwise, I would not have bothered to call you."

They arranged to meet at a downtown café. Richard said he would carry a red rose so she could identify him. I took my boys to Sophia's so I could babysit her kids while she went to meet Richard. Sophia arranged her dark hair to frame her beautiful face, and applied a discreet amount of makeup. She put on an attractive outfit that complemented her curves, along with high heels. I urged her to be careful and to call me if she encountered any trouble.

After less than two hours, my cellphone rang. Sophia was driving home. "You won't believe it," she said, laughing so hard I was worried she would lose control of her steering wheel. Later, while the kids watched a movie, Sophia told me her story.

"When I entered the café, I saw a man with a red rose sitting at a table with his back to the door. As I approached, he turned to me and stood up. I was so shocked I almost fell over! He was about five-foot-five with a very dark complexion, a protuberant belly, and a tuft of hair, twisted from the back of his head to his forehead to cover his bald scalp. He was really, really unattractive, and probably in his mid or late sixties. Richard pulled out a chair for me and ordered us coffee. I tried to listen politely to his small talk about his business, and about being from the Middle East. Though I wanted to end this encounter as quickly as possible, Richard insisted that he thought we had 'hit it right.'"

Sophia replied, "I'm sorry, I do not have the same impression. Do you really feel you fit the person you described to me?'"

"Absolutely," he said.

Sophia thanked Richard for the coffee and told him she had to leave. "I barely made it to my car—I thought I was going to piss my pants laughing!"

We both wondered what had been going on in Richard's head. Did he believe his lies? Did he suffer from some bizarre psychological disorder? Sophia removed her newspaper ad the next day. Instead, she joined an Italian internet dating site. After four months of meeting people who were unattractive and/or untruthful, she gave that up as well.

I also tried my luck with a newspaper ad. Though it ran for only two weekends, I received twenty-one letters from men of all ages, some much younger than me and some much older. Some were professionals but there was also a jail guard, a farmer, a poet, a medical student, an environmentalist, and one who was unemployed. Some had typed their responses, some had handwritten letters, and one had scrawled his message on an oil-stained paper napkin. Another guy indicated that he specialized in sexual massage, describing his skills, and providing a phone number where he could be reached between 6 and 7 p.m. three nights a week.

Yet another sent a small card with the notation "applying for the job" that I was supposedly advertising. I saved each of these responses in a tidy folder—perhaps someday they could make it into another book. Only three responses seemed worth answering. I met each of these men at a café or a restaurant, but none was the companion I was seeking.

The Real Thing

Life presents many strange twists. None of my organized efforts to find a mate led anywhere, but luck did. I met my second husband,

Norm, during Christmas of 2000 while searching for an artist to create illustrations for my popular science book, *Beyond Pain*. I again placed an ad in a big daily newspaper, a professional ad this time. Ironically, it brought me the personal answer I had been seeking.

Norm was an artist who also held a full-time job in the printing shop of a large daily newspaper, the same newspaper where I had placed my personal ad. We arranged to meet in a shopping mall to discuss my project. The guy who approached me was unlike anyone I had ever met. He was taller than me, slim, with long hair tied in a ponytail that reached to his waist. He wore a gold earring and his arms were covered with tattoos. He was wearing a pair of jeans, a leather jacket with tassels, and a collarless shirt.

"A hippie!" I told myself. I expected the meeting would take twenty minutes.

That twenty minutes extended into several hours. I was attracted to Norm's warmth, his straightforward manner, the frank way he introduced himself as "an eternal rocker." In the few weeks it took for Norm to complete my illustrations, we developed a strong bond, despite the fact that he failed to check most of the boxes on the list Sophia and I had created. His qualities, which trumped all my "requirements," were his security in himself and his ability to laugh from the heart.

After Norm and I started dating, he accompanied me to a big dinner party hosted by the University of Toronto Department of Medicine. Because Norm, with his ponytail and rocker outfit, stood out in that crowd of three-piece suits, a curious male colleague of mine asked him candidly whom he was with. When Norm mentioned my name, my colleague exclaimed, "Wow, it must be very hard on you to be with her!"

Later that evening, Norm asked me, "What in the name of God did you do to that guy for him to say such a thing?"

Since that colleague and I had exchanged little beyond a few patients, I assumed my reputation as an aggressive and outspoken woman had inspired his comment.

"Are you intimidated by who I am?" I asked Norm.

His answer came straight as an arrow. "I am proud of your achievements but when you come home, what matters to me is the woman I love and care for, not your titles or bank account."

Norm and I married less than two years after meeting. Even now, two decades later, the attitude he expressed still holds true.

Love also found Sophia when she was not looking for it. As a bridesmaid, she was paired with a friend of the groom. Charles, a tall, handsome English computer consultant, had transferred to his company's Canadian office following his divorce. After their instant mutual attraction, Charles and Sophia found they shared multiple interests and several friends. Today, they are happily married and living in the United Kingdom.

A Special Kind of Man

Inspired by Norm's attitude, I asked other friends in long-term relationships what they thought were the attributes that made men capable of partnering with successful, powerful, independent women. Loretta, the corporate executive who had been left to deal with Wife Abandonment Syndrome, gave me the most eloquent answer: "I married Peter, my 100 percent good man, when my daughters were five and seven. Twenty years later, I can still say that he is my rock. Women like us need men who are very comfortable in their own skins and secure in their personal values. They also have to like themselves. It doesn't matter if they have a similar income or education, but they have to see our merits as life partners, not as titles or wallets. It really takes a strong man to stay with a strong woman." Loretta was right.

My Israeli friend, Allan, is an internationally known scientist married to Lily, a well-known architect. Allan and I first bonded through our scientific interests and a deep respect for one another. Norm and I often socialize with Allan and Lily. When I asked Allan, over coffee at an international pain conference, what type of man can pair with a successful career woman, he repeated what Loretta had said. "They have to be secure in themselves. My wife is the one who provides a stable structure for our three kids. I have deep respect for her both professionally and as a woman."

When I pressed Allan to comment about my dating experiences with men who seemed unable to deal with intelligent, successful, and attractive women, he mentioned three internationally known neuroscientists. These were intellectual giants who had made major scientific contributions to pain research. All three had walked out of long-term relationships or marriages with career woman who possessed brilliant personalities and great looks. The first scientist then became involved with a reserved, disabled older woman. The second married a quiet, reclusive woman who never accompanied him to conferences or meetings. The third married a very young, extremely shy girl who rarely spoke at social gatherings. However, over time, this shy girl finished her university studies, bloomed socially, established herself as an independent researcher at her own laboratory, and then walked out on her controlling husband.

My colleagues' tendency to run away from smart, accomplished partners gave me much to contemplate. Since some had opened doors and windows for competent females in our professional environment, how could they behave so differently in their private lives?

It occurred to me that they might be on a double track, just like high-achieving women: self-assured at work, but needing the comfort of being the head of the family at home. Fortunately, our ingrained culture that defines masculinity in terms of superiority seems to be changing. I see younger men, my own sons included, raised in households where mothers have careers, who feel at ease with professional, outspoken girlfriends and wives.

Marianne

So far, I have discussed three kinds of male partners: those who have enough self-confidence to stay with high-achieving women, those who walk out on such relationships because of their insecurities, and those who stay with high-achieving women to use and abuse them. Since I am not prepared to grant myself and other driven women immunity, I would like to acknowledge a fourth kind of male partner: those who stay with powerful career women despite being mistreated. Marianne was born in Montreal to well-educated, English-speaking parents who moved to Toronto when she started high school. Marianne and her sister graduated from private schools and then sailed through university with honors.

I met Marianne while trying to establish a Greek school in my neighborhood. A business-savvy dynamo, Marianne held an important job with the local board of education. Tall, emotional, and boisterous, she was an imposing woman who dominated her quiet and calm engineer husband, Larry. Since the couple had two sons around the same age as mine, our families began to socialize, particularly for birthday parties and other family events. This relationship started when I was still married to my first husband, and my friendship with Marianne continued after my divorce. We spoke to each other often about our personal and professional lives. Marianne liked to boast that she made grown men "weak in the knees" during business meetings. I also inferred that she had been romantically involved for years with the chair of the school board. She assisted him with their multimillion-dollar budget and implied that she was the brains behind some of the board's major projects.

Marianne carried this domineering attitude home with her, often putting down and cutting off her husband during conversations. I sometimes wondered if Larry knew about her affair. Surely, he must have suspected, given her late nights and constant phone calls with the boss. Even during our kids' birthday parties, she would sometimes retreat to another room to speak to him on her cellphone.

When the school board restructured, Marianne's boss dropped her like a dirty towel. She was emotionally demolished, as she reported to me the news of her dismissal. "How could he do this to me? I made him what he is, and put my family in jeopardy to do it!"

Marianne felt betrayed, cheated, and used. She burst into tears. The powerful woman I knew was broken. Larry remained at his wife's side during her meltdown and throughout her major depression. A year later, when Marianne took a job in the United States, Larry gave up his business to follow the woman he adored, as he had always done. Then, while she built her career, he stayed home for a couple of years to look after the kids.

Fifteen years later, the two are still together. Marianne holds an important position at a large American educational institution with the expectation of becoming dean or president of a university. Larry has returned to engineering and seems content. Five years ago, I visited the couple when I was attending a pain conference in their state. Marianne seemed a touch mellower, while Larry was the same calm and subdued man he had always been. As I observed their interaction with their grownup kids, I realized that gentle, pushed-around Larry was the strong one. He had held their family together during Marianne's personal and professional storms. He was the one the kids adored and respected. He was the one to whom Marianne turned in times of need. I hope that Marianne has learned to respect the man who stood by her and that she is grateful for her good fortune to be with him.

In my lifetime, I have witnessed a stream of generational changes between men and women in the Western world. We high-achieving women, now between forty and sixty, built on the work of earlier pioneers to break through conventional barriers to pursue everything we wanted. This meant combining marriage, motherhood, and a career. It took a lot out of us. Somewhere along the way, some of us failed a part of ourselves. Meanwhile, the men of our generation, confused and sometimes anguished by the fast pace of change, managed gender correctness in the boardroom while at times remaining rigid in their personal attitudes.

As I finished my peer research for this book, I began to wonder what legacy we had left our daughters. I assumed it was a positive one but I needed to explore this issue to be sure.

CHAPTER 9

Do Our Daughters Know Better?

A RE TODAY'S INDEPENDENT, career-driven women falling into the same traps as many of us older high-achieving women did? Surely, we must have left a positive legacy. All the women I described in this book belonged to one of the first generations to reap the benefits of the feminist movement. We set sail from home early, often leaving behind mothers who were full-time homemakers. We enrolled in universities and carved out careers by competing directly with male colleagues. Many of us became primary or sole providers who raised our kids, paid for their education, and took care of aging parents at the same time.

Our "invasion," particularly into the professions, changed the dynamics of the workplace, leading to paid maternity leave and more flexible hours. Though these shifts caused some men to target us with aggression, surely the thrust of workplace change has also created an ideological domestic shift for the next generation. None of this evolution took place in secret. Today's young women have been warned throughout their lives about abuse. They learn about it in school. They read about it in the press. They are aware of support groups that deal with it. Surely, they would at least discuss any problems they encountered with their friends.

I formulated what I thought to be a logical hypothesis: today's educated North American women are less likely than my generation, in our forties to sixties, to be subjected to abuse by a partner because now they know better. I felt confident this would prove true, if only I could figure out how to research it.

The Questionnaire

To test my hypothesis, I constructed a questionnaire (see Appendix B) to anonymously gather information from women, aged eighteen to thirty-six. As a professional researcher, I must clarify that this questionnaire was a casual, informal tool and by no means a true scientific instrument. But regardless of its limitations, I believed it would provide a glimpse into the world of young professional women and their relationships.

In the preamble to my questionnaire, I explained that I was writing a book about the abusive domestic relationships of many older high-achieving women, with my own failed marriage and experience as the focal point. I then stated my hypothesis, not hiding my expectation that more women in this generation would have traveled a smoother road than successful women in my generation. I asked first for demographic information: the responder's country of birth, her parents' country of birth, her living arrangements while growing up, her educational history, and her career history. This was to give me an idea of the subject's cultural and family milieu, ensuring that I was capturing the specific population sample that interested me.

In the second part of my questionnaire, I provided an explicit description of the signs and symptoms of physical and emotional abuse and then asked specific questions. Have you ever been in an abusive relationship? If so, what kind of abuse: physical, emotional, sexual, or a combination? Are you still in an abusive relationship? What were the circumstances of your family while growing up (parents divorced or separated; fights at home; physical, emotional, or sexual abuse; sick or addicted family member, and so on)? Do you personally know any women who are in abusive relationships? How common do you think abuse is in your circle of friends and relatives?

Finally, I posed a simple, straightforward question inviting free comment: Do you think your generation of women would tolerate physical/emotional abuse? Explain your answer, and add any comments you think are important.

This questionnaire was reviewed by several members of my staff (all mature, professional women of different ethnic backgrounds, with teenaged or adult children). I tweaked it as suggested and then showed it to some young professional women for their input. Once I had also incorporated their feedback, I made sixty copies, put them in stamped, self-addressed envelopes, and passed them along to my staff and my sons to give to young, educated women. They were variously distributed to a church congregation, a group of young teachers, employees of a downtown computer store, university students, and members of a fitness gym. Because their answers were anonymous, I could not tell which responses came from any of the above groups.

The Shocker

Thirty of the questionnaires were returned to me, a response rate of 50 percent, which is pretty good. The age of the responders ranged from nineteen to thirty-six, with twenty-six as the average. Twenty-five of the women were born in Canada, three in Europe, and one each in Iran and India, but all were raised in Canada from a very young age. Only nine had parents who were both born in Canada.

In other words, two-thirds of the women were first-generation Canadians, which is not unusual for this country. This meant either one or both of their parents were born abroad, perhaps bringing with them strong ethnic traditions from, say, Southern Europe (Italy, Portugal, Greece, Cyprus) or the Middle East or India.

As to living arrangements, half of the women were still at home, a third were living with a romantic partner, and the rest with a roommate. Two-thirds of the women were in the workforce; a quarter were attending school, and a couple were doing both. The vast majority had a university or postgraduate education; a few were in college or still in grade twelve. Their occupations included teacher, fitness instructor, retail manager, bank employee, senior analyst, team leader / customer service, massage therapist, payroll administrator, property manager, and business manager. Finally, two-thirds were involved in a relationship.

And now, we come to the core of this pilot research. Surely, these young, well-educated, Canadian-raised, professionals were less prone to abuse than my older generations.

Wrong.

Fourteen out of the thirty women, or nearly one in two—indicated that they had been in an abusive relationship. Four of the women had had more than two abusive relationships, and two were still in an abusive relationship.

Half of these women who admitted to abuse had been abused not only emotionally but physically. Of those who had terminated the relationship, more than half had initiated the split. For the remainder, separation had either been mutual or initiated by the abusive partner. Three of the women were survivors of child sexual abuse, three had had an alcoholic parent or other family member, five reported "lots of fights at home," and two had taken care of a sick or infirm family member during their childhood. In some situations, several of these conditions coexisted.

I delved deeper, trying to identify differences between the four-teen women who had been or were still being abused, and the sixteen who had never experienced partner abuse. Age, education level, or career did not seem to create the difference, but trends did emerge. The overwhelming majority of women who had been abused had immigrant parents, compared to only half of the never-abused women. Fifty percent of abused women were in relationships as compared to 80 percent of never-abused women. Only a few of the abused women currently in relationships lived with their partner, compared to all of the attached never-abused women.

This data raised a number of questions. Do abused women avoid relationships? Alternatively, did they fall into abusive relationships because they lived in strict, traditional family environments and had no dating experience? Does a restricted environment force young women to stay home even when they are in a relationship? In other words, does a strict, traditional upbringing by itself confer vulner-ability for abuse on many fronts?

The latter question popped up repeatedly in the data. So far, I have tried to point out the differences between abused and never-abused young women. Striking similarities between them emerged as well. A surprising 70 percent of the abused women and 60 per-cent of the never-abused reported they personally knew a woman who was the object of some form of abuse. Strangely, when asked whether they thought abuse was common in their circle of friends and acquaintances, the vast majority of both the abused and never-abused women reported that they did not think abuse was common.

So, what is going on here? Do abused and never-abused women alike continue to think all incidents of abuse that they witness or experience are rare occurrences, just aberrations? I was dumbfounded.

As I repeatedly pored over the survey responses, I felt as if I had been hit on the head. This feeling was not mine alone. I asked my psychologist friend, Tony, and several female colleagues to guess the percentage of modern women in this little study who admitted they had been abused. All of them guessed between 10 and 15 percent. All goggled in disbelief when I shared the numbers I had recorded.

My hypothetical constructs had been thrown into the air like a deck of cards. How had so many young women, most of them born in Canada, and all of them raised here, fallen into the same trap as we older high-achieving women?

The Failed Hypothesis

Next, I read through the written comments responding to my hypothesis that young professional women today were less likely than previous generation to be involved in abusive relationships. What a revelation. The abused women disagreed with the hypothesis and invariably gave me a list of abuse factors, along with reasons why it was propagated. An overwhelming majority of the never-abused women supported my hypothesis. However, some of them offered thoughtful explanations of circumstances that might facilitate abuse.

First, let's look at the reasons abused women cited to explain why they stayed in such relationships, and why young women today are just as likely to be abused as my generation:

- Women desire, or have been taught to desire, feeling wanted and loved, and they perceive emotional abuse as love and care.
- The cultural milieu of abused women may be oppressive or unsupportive.
- Women blame themselves for causing the abuse.
- Low self-esteem, due to a poor or troubled upbringing, is an important underlying factor.
- Strong emotional ties with the partner cause women to downplay their abuse.

- Women may stay in an abusive relationship for fear of not being able to find another partner, or because they are insecure or dependent on the abusive partner.

These additional points came up several times, and were cited by both abused and never-abused women:

- Lack of social support from friends and family is crucial in facilitating abuse.
- Women are not aware of what abuse is, particularly the emotional kind.
- Low self-esteem due to early exposure to sex, coupled with the media's promotion of carefree sexuality, leads to abuse.

One of the women, still in an abusive relationship, offered the somber observation that abuse is not isolated to any particular generation.

On the other hand, the majority of never-abused women cited these reasons why they believed abuse does not occur as often today:

- Increased awareness of abuse and the existence of helplines, support systems, and other resources for abused women.
- Significant shifts in social and cultural norms stating what is acceptable for women in relationships.
- Acceptance of being single, which leads to much less pressure on women to marry, as compared to the 1950s and 1960s.
- Higher value placed by women on career and education, facilitating financial independence and self-confidence, decreasing the likelihood of getting married "for the sake of getting married."

The reasons never-abused women cited for today's young women staying in abusive relationships were identical to those cited by the abused women.

One point that came up repeatedly from both abused and never-abused responders was the suggestion that exposure to sex, drugs, and alcohol at an early age and the promotion of carefree sexuality in popular media, such as television and films, contributes to low self-esteem. This idea was new to me, and none of the women of my generation made mention of it. But definitely it has become one of today's significant issues.

Mary

One of the unidentified young women who took my survey asked me to publish her story, which she detailed in her questionnaire. Born in Canada to Canadian parents, twenty-five-year-old Mary was a full-time student working toward her PhD. She admitted to knowing little about the signs of physical and emotional abuse before reading my definitions. Mary marked the following symptoms and signs in connection with her current partner:

- Making angry or threatening gestures
- Name-calling, mocking, accusing, blaming, yelling, swearing
- Sulking, telling me what to do
- Using "logic" to convince me I am wrong
- Not listening or responding; twisting my words; putting me down in front of other people
- Saying bad things about my friends and family
- Lying and withholding information
- Not taking a fair share of responsibility
- Not expressing his feelings; not respecting my feelings, rights, or opinions
- Shifting responsibility for abusive behavior

Mary's parents were divorced and one family member was an alcoholic. Many family fights had occurred, resulting in Mary's being both physically and emotionally abused. She also had to care for an invalid family member while growing up.

Mary knew of at least one other abused woman, but unlike other responders, avoided describing her. This made me wonder if she was referring to a close relative such as her mother or sister. She said she did not know if abuse was occurring in her circle of friends and acquaintances. When asked if she would intervene if someone she knew was being abused, she said she would if it was physical, but she was not so sure if it was emotional.

Finally, a multiple-choice question in my survey asked how would you deal with an abusive partner? Would you leave, would you seek help, or would you try to work it out with your partner? Mary indicated that she would try to work things out. Her handwritten comments were invaluable. She noted, "First, this survey is very one-sided. Men should be taking it, too. Now that I know all the things that are considered emotional abuse, I think I can be emotionally abusive to my partner, too! I also think the younger generation is more tolerant of abuse because they place so much emphasis on sex, and being sexually desirable, that they downplay the emotional aspects of relationships and perceive sex as love."

Mary's tough childhood was clearly a direct factor in her victimization as an adult. Though hers was a heart-breaking story, I felt some optimism and hope for her. Perhaps taking the questionnaire had opened her eyes to her own abuse. Perhaps she would move forward, having learned something of value from her bad choice.

As for Mary's mention of abused men, I mentioned in chapter 4 the 1999 General Social Survey on victimization involving nearly 26,000 Canadians. According to the GSS, 8 percent of women and 7 percent of men had experienced some form of abuse (physical, emotional, or sexual) at the hands of a spouse or partner. I have also related the story of Marianne, an abusive wife to obliging Larry. The fact that abused men are not the focus of this book in no way downplays their suffering.

Interpretations and Caveats

My modest, informal project (carried out around 2013) was too small to suggest the percentage of all modern professional Canadian women who are abused. As a researcher, I am careful not to overinterpret data. But it did confirm that some young women do fall into the same trap as my generation and for many of the same reasons, although I have to be cautious. Perhaps my responders exaggerated and overreported, interpreting minor spats as emotional abuse. Some could have been confused by the questionnaire. By mere chance, the survey sample may have contained an unusually large number of women who had been abused, or perhaps more of the abused were interested in completing the survey.

No matter how my findings are interpreted, I cannot avoid suspecting that partner abuse remains a problem of great severity. That was something neither I nor my colleagues had expected. This astonishing and disturbing result motivated me to delve further into what factors continue to fuel abuse despite all the progress Western women seem to have achieved.

The Next Wave of Feminism?

Certainly, our world has changed rapidly and significantly over the past three to four decades, beginning with an increase in the education women now receive in comparison to their male peers. According to the U.S. National Center for Education Statistics, 33 percent more women than men graduated from American colleges in 2012. The U.S. Department of Education suggests this figure will increase to 47 percent by 2023. As one would expect, higher education leads to more remunerative work, so it is no longer uncommon for women to out-earn their husbands or boyfriends. Unfortunately, extensive research shows that holding a higher-status or higher-earning job "is bad for the relationship."[34]

In a study published in 2017,[35] Canadian researchers Drs. Byrne and Barling surveyed 209 high-achieving Canadian businesswomen who were in heterosexual marriages or common-law relationships, along with fifty-three of their husbands or partners. Most of the women held at least a university degree, as compared to 31 percent of their male partners, and most out-earned their partners. They found that these high-achieving women were more likely to feel their husbands' lower status decreased their own, resulting in less marital satisfaction and an increased likelihood they were contemplating divorce. Significantly, when the wives felt their husbands provided them with high levels of support (household chores, child and elder care), their higher-status positions did not affect their marital satisfaction.

The researchers also commented that some women might choose to downplay their careers so as not to threaten their partners, or even to abandon their high-status careers in exchange for "happiness at home." A *Refinery29* article on an anonymous 2015 survey of high-earning millennial women found that 38 percent of American wives earned more than their husbands and that many of these women reported that earning more threatened their relationships. In keeping with the reports of Drs. Byrne and Barling, the survey found that many high-achieving women felt especially unappreciated by their spouses if they returned home from demanding jobs to an overabundance of household chores.[36] There are suggestions that women have been socialized to invest more care into these chores than men, and that they are disproportionately expected to bear the weight of household duties and childcare.[37] Judith Shulevitz asserts that women are the "designated worrier" of the household and that they are expected to maintain "large reserves of emotional energy to stay on top of it all."[38]

In the *New York Times*, Stephanie Coontz reported on several studies that showed that millennial men (born between 1982 and 2000) were more likely than the previous generation to want a stay-at-home wife. An obvious explanation is that many, having lost dominance in the workplace, need to feel dominance on the home front. However, another explanation may be that American men, lacking the social policies that support work-family balance in European societies (such as France, Germany, the Netherlands, Sweden, and Norway) prefer the more traditional family arrangement because it is less stressful.[39]

Many other studies support the concept that male loss of dominance can lead to domestic troubles. In a report published in 2013,[40] the University of Chicago Booth School of Business looked at four thousand married U.S. couples. When a wife earned more than her husband (and it did not matter if it was a little more or a lot), divorce rates increased. More startlingly, women who were primary earners did more housework than other wives. In their analysis, the researchers felt that that the higher-earning women were trying to prevent their husbands from feeling emasculated by their career success.

A study of young American couples (married and unmarried) from Cornell University[41] found that the more a man was financially dependent on his partner, the more likely he was to cheat on her. The author explained this phenomenon as the male need to conform to society's definitions of masculinity; in these cases, a man's "infidelity may be an attempt to restore relationship equity" and regain a sense of power.[42]

In data collected in 2013 from 200,000 married Danish couples, researchers from Washington University found that women earning more than their spouses were more likely to use medications for anxiety and to suffer sleep problems.[43]

Here is the bottom line: multiple streams of evidence reveal that as women advance in education, job status, and financial achievements, they are likely to encounter more domestic trouble. Married women with higher-status jobs are referred to as having "married down," which is an attitude they themselves may hold. They are more likely to be victims of their husbands' resentful aggression and are at higher risk of divorce, whether it is sought by themselves or by their spouses.

Perhaps dealing with this intensifying issue may define the next wave of feminism. If so, the realignment of male/female expectations will have to be an initiative of both genders. As I discovered with my own pilot study of young women, when it comes to actual domestic abuse more factors are at play than just education and job status. While these may set the stage for some troubled marriages, the willingness for a woman to accept abuse as "normal" also depends on her upbringing, her life experiences, her personality, her psychosocial circumstances, and so forth.

Another factor that puts today's young women at greater risk than before, suggested by my pilot study, was my participants' repeated comment that exposure to sex, drugs, and alcohol at an early age and the promotion of carefree sexuality in popular media contribute to a young woman's low self-esteem. A quick look at many music videos, magazines, and advertisements shows more than ever how intensely and repeatedly young women are objectified. Popular singers, from Madonna to Britney Spears and Beyoncé, sport scanty outfits with camera angles hyping their sexuality. While they may claim to be promoting "girl power" by flaunting it, in reality they give confusing and conflicting messages to young women, implying that their worth is based solely on their bodies and the males they can attract. This, as my young responders pointed out, fosters low self-esteem, which can lead to eating disorders, anxiety, depression, and other psychological problems.

Culture and Abuse

The strongest implication arising from my data, both for my own generation and for the younger women who participated in my survey, is that cultural and ethnic upbringing is a significant factor conferring vulnerability for abuse. As an immigrant myself, I experienced a similar strict upbringing, a superficial level of communication with my parents, and societal norms allowing men to "scream" at women just because they were men. So did many other high-achieving women in this book. One of my graduate trainees, a Muslim from a wealthy Pakistani business family who was working toward her PhD, told me that many of her friends would likely have marked several symptoms of abuse while still believing they were not being abused due to strikingly different cultural norms.

Canada is a country of immigrants, and the sources of immigration are changing. Prior to 1960, the vast majority of immigrants came from Europe, including many southern Europeans with strict family traditions. Today, most Canadian immigrants come from the Philippines, India, Pakistan, China, and Hong Kong, and they are coming in great numbers. A 2010 Statistics Canada survey[44] estimates that by 2031, 46 per cent of all Canadians over the age of fifteen will either be foreign-born or have at least one foreign-born parent. For better or worse, these new waves of immigrants will bring cultural and religious traditions of their own. While acknowledging that there is very little research on the topic, I think it is reasonable to ask how they will reconcile themselves to Canada's liberalized environment. How will young, professional women from these cultures grow up in North America? Will their cultures, traditions, and religious beliefs continue to shape the way they relate to men? Will they experience the same, different, or worse vulnerabilities than we earlier immigrants experienced? And as more of these women become CEOs, physicians, lawyers, business owners, what parts of their culture will they bring to the professional/corporate environment and what part to their families?

It is important to keep in mind that it is difficult to force major change within an ethnic or cultural milieu. Usually, only acculturation over generations can do this. New ethnic voices like that of the human rights activist Samra Zafar are helping. Samra, who came from Pakistan to live with her husband in Canada several years ago, has just published *A Good Wife: Escaping The Life I Never Chose*, a heart-breaking story of her arranged and abusive marriage. There is also a documentary film, *Because We Are Girls*, about three Punjabi-Canadian sisters who were sexually-abused by a relative. This film is making its debut at the 2019 Hot Docs festival in Toronto.

All of us have both a huge opportunity and a social responsibility to better educate young North American women, irrespective of their cultural backgrounds, about the definition of abuse, particularly in its subtler emotional form. Educators, administrators, and policy makers must take serious note. Proper education should start in the home and continue in elementary and high schools, in post-secondary educational institutions, in all places of worship, in social media, and in the workplace. A concerted effort is both feasible and necessary so that our daughters, and our sons' partners, need not repeat the suffering so many of us experienced.

EPILOGUE

MORE THAN THIRTY YEARS have passed since that September morning in 1986 when I brought newborn Alex home from the hospital. The tears of that day (and of many days before and after) have long since dried, and my unhappy first marriage has been put into perspective. Now that its painful lessons that are imprinted on my brain have found their way into this book, I feel my journey has come to a satisfying conclusion. Yet, I still wonder what happened to the other women whose stories I shared, the ones who were only partway into their journeys when we last met?

One Sunday morning, five years ago, Norm and I were again visiting our local coffee shop, which was abuzz with many others enjoying their morning caffeine fix. A woman's voice greeted me warmly from the other side of the room. As its owner sauntered in our direction, I squinted against the sun's glare, trying to focus on her face.

It was Gordana, the friend Norm and I used to meet here many moons ago, along with her husband, Andrei. I had not seen her for several years, since her participation in the 2008 forum at my home and her subsequent meeting with me where she disclosed the years of abuse she had endured at the hands of her husband. Gordana pulled up a chair and began updating me on her life, bubbling with excitement, and comfortably including Norm, whom she viewed as a wise man. Whereas Gordana used to be secretive about Andrei's abuse, now she openly related a particular incident, which had occurred a few months after she had attended the forum.

A colleague had asked Gordana about a sizable rectangular bruise on her chest, which Gordana had attributed to dropping a dumbbell on herself while exercising. In fact, Andrei had thrown the television converter box at her, leaving this imprint. Why was he so angry? She had confronted him about a long-term affair that she had just discovered. Gordana had spent the next hour sobbing in her car, distraught by her inability to deal with Andrei's abuse. With her face puffy from crying, she told her reflection in the visor mirror, "You do not deserve this—not the cheating, not the beating, and not the humiliation."

This was Gordana's defining moment. That evening, she informed her teenaged son, who had been urging her to leave the marriage, that now she was ready. She placed an urgent call to a cousin in her home-land, urging her to come to Canada, to stay with her and Andrei as a buffer while she took the necessary steps to end their relationship. Gordana filed for separation. She told Andrei their marriage was over, with her cousin and son standing beside her for support.

For several months, the couple cohabited, with Andrei in the basement during the brief periods he was not long-haul trucking to the United States. Once Gordana seized the upper hand, Andrei's behavior changed dramatically. For almost a year, he was friendly and soft, hoping they could reconcile. His optimism was misplaced. He had already lost both Gordana and his son, who refused to talk to him. He had also lost some of former friends, as the truth behind the couple's separation became known.

Once the divorce papers were finalized, Andrei was forced to leave the family home and to find an apartment of his own. As Gordana related her story, she spoke quickly, taking short breaths, trying to squeeze as much information into as short a time as possible. She seemed airy and confident, different than I remembered her.

"I'm dating now," she announced, "but this time I pick and choose. I will not tolerate anyone who whines, complains, who seems controlling, or needs to be pampered. I've paid my dues. They will have to pamper me, and respect me, the way I deserve."

Before Gordana hurried off to work (now, as a full-time manager of a high-end women's fashion store), she gave me a big hug, fervently thanking me and leaving a wake of confidence and strength. I thought about the fact that it was the sight of her tearful face in her car mirror that had helped her to confront the suffering self she had been hiding. That mirroring had begun with my forum where she had realized she was not alone. All of us that evening had seen parts of ourselves in each other's stories as we verbalized our feelings, some for the first time. I was sure, now, that when Gordana looked at her reflection, she would continue to see her new strength and vitality. I also felt gratified to know that my difficult journey, in researching this book, was already paying small dividends to women who had participated. This gave me hope that the abuse survey that I had circulated among younger women would also help them to begin to understand their own sad truths.

Unfortunately, nothing I could ever say or do could help Elana Fric-Shamji, whose untimely death spurred me to finish this book and continues to haunt my memory. Even after the media discontinued their regular updates, reminders continued to circulate among colleagues in my own hospital. With the dishonorable departure of Mo Shamji, Elana's husband, from the University Health Network, his name became an uncomfortable topic of discussion. Even now, scarcely a week goes by that a patient, a hospital friend, or a colleague fails to bring up Elana's cruel death in disbelief.

Mo Shamji was the son of a prominent thoracic surgeon and a psychiatrist mother, distinguished members of the Ismaili Muslim community. Elana, the daughter of hard-working Croatian immigrants, was a precociously talented, very smart child who fulfilled her dream of becoming a doctor. Throughout Elana's twelve-year marriage, she had endured verbal, emotional, and physical abuse. Her parents knew, many of her friends knew, and Mo's parents probably knew. Typically, in the couple's Facebook posts, they presented themselves as a subject of envy—fun-loving, affectionate, and blessed with wonderful children.

After Elana's death, the Ontario Medical Association released a link to a website (www.canadianwomen.org/violence-prevention-resources) with eight tips on how to assist someone you know is involved in an abusive relationship. These tips were created by the Canadian Women's Foundation in partnership with women's shelters and transition houses:

1. Be supportive in a non-judgmental manner.
2. Educate yourself about relationship violence.
3. Be aware of the risks so that the way you communicate with the victim does not put that person in greater danger.
4. Ensure your own safety since confrontation with the abuser may place you at risk.
5. Locate resources before speaking with the victim.
6. Choose the right time and place to communicate with the victim.
7. Voice your concerns to the victim in a sensitive way.
8. Put the victim in charge by exploring options with her.

In September 2017, Mo Shamji was denied bail, after relatives of Elana packed the court to hear the judge's decision. Elana's parents had asked the court to freeze the couple's assets and to permit sale of the matrimonial home to pay for huge bills for lawyers and for custody issues, as well as for taking care of Elana's children, who live with them in Windsor.

On the eve of his trial in April, 2019 Mo Shamji plead guilty to the second-degree murder of his wife. In a poem entitled "Shattered

Glass," which Elana wrote as a teenager, she revealed the lack of self-worth, so common to abused women:

> My reflection stares
> into my eyes.
> A useless girl
> whom I despise.[45]

Yes, Elana was one of us, conquering the boardroom but hiding at home. Some of us were able to escape. Elana, like too many others, did not make it to safety, though she fought till her last breath.

APPENDIX A: RESOURCES

Canada

Status of Women Canada
Canadian Women's Health Network
The National Clearinghouse on Family Violence
The Canadian Clearinghouse on Cyberstalking
Canadian Women's Foundation
Women's Shelters Canada
Shelter Safe
Springtide Resources
Kanawayhitowin: Taking Care of Each Other's Spirit

United States

The National Coalition Against Domestic Violence
The National Women's Health Information Center, operated by the
    Office on Women's Health
U.S. Department of Justice Office on Violence Against Women
The Family Violence Prevention and Services Program
Mental Health America
Neighbours, Friends & Families

APPENDIX B: QUESTIONNAIRE

The following is the anonymous questionnaire sent out to women aged eighteen to thirty-six.

Background

My name is Angela Mailis Gagnon. I am a medical doctor and Professor of Medicine at the University of Toronto. I am writing a book on professional women who get involved in bad personal relationships and suffer greatly at home while they maintain a successful career or work outside the home, living a "dual" existence. A major factor in these unequal relationships is emotional abuse (and sometimes physical abuse) to which these women are subjected. I know, because I was one of them. I have collected many stories of such women in their 40s and 50s living in North America.

However, my personal feeling is that acceptance of such bad relationships is not tolerated well by younger educated women in their 20s and 30s. I also have the feeling that young men are changing and participate more in family and household chores while they have a greater respect for their female partners. By you answering this questionnaire you help me better understand the issue of abuse as seen and experienced through women of the new generation. I have two sons and have often wondered if I had a daughter how she would consider these issues. Your answers can give me a better understanding of how women of the twenty-first century respond to this serious topic.

Please be assured that you will fill this questionnaire anonymously. I will be more than happy to deliver to you a synopsis of the young women who answer this questionnaire.

PLEASE READ THIS BEFORE YOU FILL
THE QUESTIONNAIRE BELOW:

Warning signs of emotional and physical abuse and the behaviors associated with them are listed by Peace at Home, a human rights agency that addresses not only the severity of domestic violence but calls attention to signs of abuse. The signs and behaviors listed below tend to be perpetually repeated and are usually manifested in multiples, with women experiencing many such signs simultaneously.

Acts of violence (physical abuse)

1. Intimidation: Making angry or threatening gestures; use of physical size to intimidate; standing in doorway during arguments; shouting at partner; driving recklessly.
2. Destruction: Destroying your possessions (e.g. furniture); punching walls; throwing and/or breaking things.
3. Threats: Making and/or carrying threats to hurt you or others.
4. Sexual violence: Degrading treatment based on your sex or sexual orientation; using force or coercion to obtain sex or perform sexual acts.
5. Physical violence: Being violent to you, your children, household pets or others; slapping; punching; grabbing; kicking; choking; pushing; biting; stabbing; shooting etc.

6. Weapons: Use of weapons, keeping weapons around that frighten you; threatening or attempting to kill you or those you love.

Emotional abuse

1. Destructive criticism / verbal abuse: Name-calling; mocking; accusing; blaming; yelling; swearing; making humiliating remarks or gestures.
2. Pressure tactics: Rushing you to make decisions through "guilt-tripping" and other forms of intimidation; sulking; threatening to withhold money; manipulating the children; telling you what to do.
3. Abusing authority: Always claiming to be right (insisting statements are "the truth"); making decisions without consulting partner; using "logic" against partner for one's own gain.
4. Disrespect: Interrupting; changing topics; not listening or responding; twisting your words; putting you down in front of other people; saying bad things about your friends and family.
5. Abusing trust: Lying; withholding information; cheating on you; being overly jealous.
6. Breaking promises: Not following through on agreements; not taking a fair share of responsibility; refusing to help with childcare or housework.
7. Emotional withholding: Not expressing feelings; not giving support, attention, or compliments; not respecting feelings, rights, or opinions.
8. Minimizing, denying, and blaming: Making light of behavior and not taking your concerns seriously; saying the abuse did not happen; shifting responsibility for abusive behavior; saying you caused it.

9. Economic control: Interfering with partner's work or not letting partner work; refusing to give you or taking your money; taking your car keys or otherwise preventing you from using the car; threatening to report you to welfare or other social agencies.

10. Self-destructive behavior: Abusing drugs or alcohol; threatening suicide or other forms of self-harm; deliberately saying or doing things that have negative consequences (e.g., telling your boss).

11. Isolation: Preventing or making it difficult for you to see friends or relatives; monitoring phone calls; telling you where you can and cannot go.

12. Harassment: Making uninvited visits or calls; following you; checking up on you; embarrassing you in public; refusing to leave when asked.

Now that you have read the signs of physical and emotional abuse, please fill the questionnaire below.

Q1. How old are you? _____

Q2. Which city and country were you born? _____
_____

Q3. Please report the country of birth for

your mother _____ and
your father _____

Q4. What is your living accommodation?

Home with parents / immediate family_____;
Live with roommate_____;
Live with romantic partner (married or common-law)_____;
Live alone_____

Q5. What exactly are you doing now?

Work_____;   Both_____;
Go to school_____;   Neither_____

Q6. What is the highest level of education you have achieved?

Elementary school_____;
High school_____;
College_____;
University / undergraduate studies_____;
Postgraduate studies_____

Q7. If you are working now, what is your occupation?

_____

Q8. Are you currently in any relationship? Yes _____ No _____

Q9. What was your knowledge of physical/emotional abuse before filling this questionnaire?

Not knowledgeable about the signs_____
Somewhat knowledgeable about the signs_____
Very knowledgeable about the signs_____

Q10. BASED ON WHAT YOU READ ABOVE, have you ever been involved in an abusive relationship? Yes _____ No _____

IF YOUR ANSWER IS NO, PLEASE GO TO QUESTION #16

Q11. If your answer is YES, please CONTINUE TO SCORE the signs of abuse list above by marking with a circle all those signs that apply to you and then report the number of abuse signs below.

# of physical abuse signs ___ # of emotional abuse signs ___

Q12. Are you still in this abusive relationship? Yes _____ No _____

If you answered No, please respond to the following question:

Q13. Who initiated the separation?

You _____ The partner _____ Was mutual decision _____

Q14. Have you been involved in more than one abusive relationships?
Yes _____ No _____

If the answer is yes, indicate how many _____

Q15. It is believed that persons who end up in abusive relationships had some kind of trouble at home. Please check all those that apply to you (even if you were not in abusive relationship).

_____parents were separated or divorced;

_____alcohol or other problems in the family;

_____lots of fights at home;

_____you were subject of physical or emotional abuse;

_____you were subject of sexual abuse,

_____you felt you were not loved;

_____you took care of an older person (parent) or sick person at home since young age;

_____lived in foster home

OTHER_____

Q16. Do you know of any friend / acquaintance / family member of yours who is / has been in an abusive relationship?

Yes _____ No _____

If you answered Yes, please describe this person better:

Her age is _____
She goes to school _____ Works _____ Both _____
If she works, her job is _____

You believe this person is subject to:

Emotional abuse _____
Physical abuse _____
Both _____

Q17. In your opinion, is physical/emotional abuse common in your circle of friends and acquaintances?

Yes_____ Seldom_____ No_____ I do not know_____

Q18. Would you know now that you have read the signs, what physical/emotional abuse is if you witnessed it?

Yes_____ No_____ Maybe_____

Q19. Would you try to intervene if you knew a friend/ acquaintance/ family member was being subjected to emotional/physical abuse? Yes _____ No _____ I am not sure _____

Q20. How do you think you would react to emotional/physical abuse if it were present in a future relationship?

I would leave_____
I would seek help from a family member or friend_____
I would try to work it out with my partner_____

Q21. Do you think the younger generation of women would tolerate physical/emotional abuse today? Explain your answer and
add any comments you think are important.

_____

_____

_____

_____

_____

_____

_____

_____

_____

_____

_____

_____

_____

_____

_____

_____

DATE YOU FILLED THE QUESTIONNAIRE _____

I want to thank you very much for taking the time and making the
effort to answer this questionnaire.

Please mail it back anonymously in the pre-stamped envelope.

For any questions or comments please do not hesitate to contact me
(phone number, fax, and email given).

ACKNOWLEDGMENTS

I WANT TO THANK, first and foremost, Anna Kenyon, my secretary of more than thirty years who was my counselor, friend, and support through the hard years of my marriage and particularly my divorce. Also Dr. Tony Hunt, my friend and colleague, who reviewed the original manuscript and offered me interpretations and priceless advice; my literary agent and friend Beverley Slopen, who supported me through the fifteen years it took me to compose this book; Sylvia Fraser, who reorganized and edited the content, making sure my voice came across as I intended; all the women I referred to in this book who entrusted me with their personal stories; the numerous friends who encouraged me to "speak out"; and, most of all, my two sons, Nicholas and Alex, grown men now and the apples of my eye, who sustained me throughout my difficult marriage and helped us become the family we are today.

NOTES

1 Marta Burczycka and Shana Conroy, *Family Violence in Canada: A Statistical Profile, 2015*, Canadian Centre for Justice Statistics, Feb. 16, 2017, cat. no. 85-002-X ISSN 1209-6393, www.statcan.gc.ca/pub/85-002-x/2017001/article/14698-eng.pdf.
2 United Nations Office on Drugs and Crime, "Global Study on Homicide 2013: Trends, Contexts, Data," 2014.
3 World Health Organization, Department of Reproductive Health and Research, "Intimate partner violence during pregnancy," 2011.
4 J. O'Neil, "Gender Role Conflict Research: New Directions to Understand Men's Violence," paper presented at the Annual Convention of the American Psychological Association, Aug. 1992, Washington, DC.
5 J. Lachkar, "Emotional Abuse of High-Functioning Professional Women," *Journal of Emotional Abuse*, 2(1), 2000, 73-91.
6 M.T. Loring, *Emotional Abuse* (New York: Lexington Books, 1994).
7 M.C. Black, K.C. Basile, M.J. Breiding, S.G. Smith, M.L. Walters, M.T. Merrick, J. Chen, and M.R. Stevens, "The National Intimate Partner and Sexual Violence Survey: 2010 Summary Report," Center for Injury Prevention and Control and Centers for Disease Control and Prevention (2011).
8 Peace at Home, *Domestic Violence: The Facts* (Boston, 1997).
9 Claire Cain Miller, "When Wives Earn More Than Husbands, Neither Partner Likes to Admit It," *New York Times*, July 17, 2018.
10 Joan Lachkar, *The Many Faces of Abuse: Treating the Emotional Abuse of High-Functioning Women* (Northvale, NJ: Jason Aronson, 1998).
11 Massachusetts Coalition of Battered Women Service Groups, "For Shelter and Beyond" (Boston, MA, 1990).
12 D.W. Winnicott, *The Maturational Processes and the Facilitating Environment* (New York: International Universities Press, 1965).

13 Mental Health America, "Co-Dependency," www.nmha.org/go/codependency.

14 Lachkar, *The Many Faces of Abuse*, 22.

15 Lachkar, *The Many Faces of Abuse*, 26–7.

16 T. Singer et al., "Empathy for Pain Involves the Affective but Not Sensory Components of Pain," *Science* 303 (2004), 1157–62.

17 Giacomo Rizzolatti and Luciano Fadiga, "Resonance Behaviors and Mirror Neurons," *Italiennes de Biologie* 137 (1999), 85–100.

18 T. Singer et al., "Empathic Neural Responses Are Modulated by the Perceived Fairness of Others," *Nature* 439 (2006), 466–9.

19 C.Y. Yang et al., "Gender Differences in the Mu Rhythm during Empathy for Pain: An Electroencephalographic Study," *Brain Research* 1251 (2009), 176–84; S. Han S., Y. Fan, and L. Mao, "Gender Difference in Empathy for Pain: An Electrophysiological Investigation," *Brain Research* 1196 (2008), 85–93.

20 S.M. Fisch, B. Homer, E. Galiardo, and S. Zabolotnaia, "Gender Differences in Empathy: A Cross-Cultural Comparison," paper presented at the annual meeting of the International Communication Association, 2009, http://citation.allacademic.com/meta/p170865_index.html.

21 D.J. Langford et al., "Social Modulation of Pain as Evidence of Empathy in Mice," *Science* 312 (2006), 1967–70.

22 Katharine Blick Hoyenga and Kermit T. Hoyenga, *Gender-Related Differences: Origins and Outcomes* (Boston: Allyn and Bacon,) 1993.

23 Louann Brizendine, *The Female Brain* (New York: Broadway Books, 2006).

24 Brizendine, *The Female Brain*, 2.

25 U.S. Senate Committee on Judiciary Hearings, Violence Against Women Act, 1990.

26 Senator Joseph Biden, U.S. Senate Committee on Judiciary Hearings, Violence Against Women: Victims of the System, 1991.

27 Yasmin Jiwani, "The 1999 General Social Survey on Victimization (GSS): An Analysis," *Canadian Woman Studies* 20, no. 3 (2000).

28 Jiwani, "The 1999 General Social Survey on Victimization".

29 http://www.phac-aspc.gc.ca/ncfv-cnivf/publications/femviol-eng.php

30 Scott M. Langevin and Karl T Kelsey, "The fate is not always written in the genes: epigenomics in epidemiologic studies," *Environmental and molecular mutagenesis* vol. 54,7 (2013), 533-41, doi:10.1002/em.21762

31 Ting Zhang, Josh Hoddenbagh, Susan McDonald, and Katie Scrim, *An Estimation of the Economic Impact of Spousal Violence in Canada, 2009* (Ottawa: Department of Justice Canada, Research and Statistics Division, 2012).

32 M. Holmes, F. Richter, M. Votruba, K. Berg, and A. Bender, "Economic Burden of Child Exposure to Intimate Partner Violence in the United States," *Journal of Family Violence*, 33, no. 4 (2018), 239-249, https://doi.org/10.1007/s10896-018-9954-7

33 Cynthia Hess and Alona Del Rosario, "Dreams Deferred: A Survey on the Impact of Intimate Partner Violence on Survivors' Education, Careers, and Economic Security," Institute for Women's Policy Research publication #C475 (2018), https://iwpr.org/publications/dreams-deferred-domestic-violence-survey-2018/

34 *Washington Post*, July 26, 2017.

35 A. Byrne and J. Barling, "When She Brings Home the Job Status: Wives' Job Status, Status Leakage, and Marital Instability," *Organizational Science*, April 4, 2017, https://doi.org/10.1287/orsc.2017.1120.

36 Ashley C. Ford, "Millennial Women are Conflicted About Being Breadwinners," *Refinery29*, (May 1, 2017), https://www.refinery29.com/en-us/2017/04/148488/millennial-women-are-conflicted-about-being-breadwinners

37 Annette Lareau and Elliot Weininger, "Time, Work, and Family Life: Reconceptualizing Gendered Time Patterns Through the Case of Children's Organized Activities," *Sociological Forum* 23, no. 3 (September 2008), 419-454

38 Judith Shulevitz, "Mom: The Designated Worrier," *New York Times*, May 8, 2015.

39 *New York Times*, March 31, 2017.

40 M. Bertrand, E. Kamenica, and J. Pan, "Gender Identity and Relative Income within Households," *Quarterly Journal of Economics* 130, no. 2 (May 1, 2015), 571–614, https://doi.org/10.1093/qje/qjv001.

41 Christin L. Munsch, "Her Support, His Support: Money, Masculinity, and Marital Infidelity," *American Sociological Review* 80 (2015), 469–95.

42 Munsch, 469

43 L. Pierce, M.S. Dahl, and J. Nielsen, "In Sickness and in Wealth: Psychological and Sexual Costs of Income Comparison in Marriage," *Personality and Social Psychology Bulletin* 39, no. 3 (2013), 359–74.

44 Statistics Canada, "Ethnic diversity and immigration," 2010, https://www150.statcan.gc.ca/n1/pub/11-402-x/2011000/chap/imm/imm-eng.htm

45 Elana Fric-Shamji, quoted in Michael Lista, "Love and Death," *Toronto Life*, May 17, 2017.